Contents

Grilled Vegetable Salad with Fresh Herb Vinaigrette 7

Healthy Garden Salad 8

Crispy Cucumbers and Tomatoes in Dill Dressing 9

Insalata Caprese II 9

Cucumber Sunomono 10

Roasted Yam and Kale Salad 10

Tangy Cucumber and Avocado Salad 11

Tomato, Basil, and Feta Salad 12

Mom's Cucumbers 12

Chickpea Salad with Red Onion and Tomato 13

Chrissy's Sweet 'n' Sour Tomato Salad 13

Broccoli-Cauliflower Salad 14

Sun-Dried Tomato Basil Orzo 14

Tomato, Cucumber and Red Onion Salad with Mint 15

Fatoosh 16

Greek Salad III 16

Owen's Mozzarella and Tomato Salad 17

Mexican Salad 18

Balsamic Pea Salad 18

Couscous and Cucumber Salad 19

Penne, Tomato, and Mozzarella Salad 20

Black Bean, Corn, and Tomato Salad with Feta Cheese 20

Fresh Tomato Salad 21

Carrot Salad 22

Sesame Broccoli Salad 22

Celery Salad 23

Hungarian Cucumber Salad 23

Raw Vegetable Salad 24

Tomato and Avocado Salad 25

Tofu Salad 25

Chinese-Style Broccoli Salad 26

Marinated Beet Salad 26

Tomato-Mint Quinoa Salad 27

Bacon Pea Salad.. 28

Cucumber Salad with Dill Vinaigrette 29

Easy Cherry Tomato Corn Salad 29

Broccoli Cauliflower Pepita Salad 30

Red Potato, Asparagus, and Artichoke Salad 31

Vegan Black Bean and Sweet Potato Salad 32

My Favorite Beet Salad.. 32

Persian-Style Tomato Avocado Salad 33

Lemon Pea Salad... 34

Marinated Cucumber, Onion, and Tomato Salad... 34

Old Fashioned Potato Salad... 35

Dad's Creamy Cucumber Salad... 36

Fresh Broccoli Salad 37

Greek Zoodle Salad... 37

Pittsburgh Football Sunday Pasta Salad 38

Grilled Cheese and Veggie Sandwich 39

Thai Chicken Slaw Burgers.. 40

Corn Salad with Creamy Italian Dressing.. 41

Corn in a Cup (Elote en Vaso) 42

Southwestern Roasted Corn Salad 43

Pasta with Fresh Tomatoes and Corn.. 44

Kate's Grilled Corn Salad 44

Roasted Corn and Heirloom Tomato Salad 45

Refreshing Cucumber Salad... 46

Bacon Avocado Salad.. 47

Red Broccoli Salad 47

Bacon Ranch Pea Salad.. 48

Almond Mandarin Salad 49

Mediterranean Greek Salad 49

Gurkensalat (German Cucumber Salad)... 50

Black Bean and Corn Salad I 50

Barb's Broccoli-Cauliflower Salad 51

Cucumber Slices With Dill 52

Garlic Broccoli 52

Broccoli Salad I 53

Green Bean and Potato Salad 53

Mexican Cucumber Salad 54

Zesty Coleslaw 55

Mediterranean Lentil Salad 55

Pesto Pasta Caprese Salad 56

Israeli Salad 57

Easy Seven Layer Vegetable Salad 57

Garlicky Beet Delight 58

Black-Eyed Pea Salad 59

Byrdhouse Marinated Tomatoes and Mushrooms 59

Spicy Italian Salad 60

Deep Dish Layered Salad 61

Cucumber and Tomato Salad 62

Spring Salad 62

Tomato Cucumber Salad II 63

Blackberry Spinach Salad 64

Asian Cucumber Salad 64

Cucumbers in Sour Cream 65

Apple Avocado Salad with Tangerine Dressing 65

Spinach Caprese Salad 66

Super Easy Spinach and Red Pepper Salad 67

Green Bean Blue Cheese Salad 67

Twenty-Four Hour Salad 68

Apple Coleslaw 68

Creamy Cauliflower Salad 69

Cilantro, Avocado, Tomato, and Feta Salad 70

Cucumber, Tomato, and Red Onion Salad 70

Cilantro Cucumber Salad 71

Tortellini Pesto Salad 71

Red Quinoa and Avocado Salad 72

Broccoli Salad 73

Cool Cucumber and Avocado Salad 73

Cucumber Salad With Thai Sweet Chili Vinaigrette 74

Tomato Mozzarella Salad 75

Easy Cucumber Salad 75

Cottage Cheese Salad 76

Broccoli Raisin Salad 76

Cucumber Salad I 77

Asian Cucumber Thai Salad 77

Amazing Cucumber Basil Salad 78

Marinated Cherry Tomato Salad 79

Summer Corn Salad 79

Grilled Corn Salad 80

Avocado Salad 81

Portable Chinese Chicken Salad 81

Chicken Mango Salsa Salad with Chipotle Lime Vinaigrette 82

Thai Chicken Broccoli Slaw 83

Beefy Cabbage Stew 84

Catfish Po Boy 85

Timesaver Kale Slaw 86

Golompke (Beef and Cabbage Casserole) 87

Thai Shrimp and Cabbage 87

Weeknight Crack Slaw 88

Grilled Corn and Red Cabbage Slaw 89

Grilled Corn Off the Cob Salad 90

Hatch Chile Corn 91

Angie's Dad's Best Cabbage Coleslaw 92

Marinated Cucumber, Onion, and Tomato Salad 92

Black Bean Salad 93

Mom's Cucumber Salad 93

Strawberry Avocado Salad 94

Roasted Beets with Feta 94

Ali's Greek Tortellini Salad 95

Avocado and Tuna Tapas 96

Caribbean Sweet Potato Salad 97

Orzo and Tomato Salad with Feta Cheese 97

Cherry Tomato Salad 98

Dave's Coleslaw 99

Tomato Cucumber Salad 99

Cilantro Tomato Corn Salad 100

Greek Pasta Salad with Shrimp, Tomatoes, Zucchini, Peppers, and Feta 101

Insalata Caprese I 102

Korean Cucumber Salad 102

Avocado and Tomato Salad 103

California Salad Bowl 103

P.J.'s Fresh Corn Salad 104

Broccoli Salad IV 105

Carrot and Raisin Salad II 105

Mediterranean Zucchini and Chickpea Salad 106

Tomato Cucumber Onion Salad 106

Tomato Cucumber Salad with Mint 107

Carmel's Crunchy Pea Salad 108

Apple and Zucchini Salad 108

Sauerkraut Salad 109

Crisp Marinated Cucumbers 109

My Big Fat Greek Salad 110

A Different Carrot Raisin Salad 111

Raw Beet Salad 112

Broccoli Salad with Red Grapes, Bacon, and Sunflower Seeds 112

Lemony Cucumbers 113

Asian Pasta Salad with Beef, Broccoli and Bean Sprouts 114

Easy Broccoli Salad 115

Grilled Asparagus Salad 116

Mexican Street Vendor Style Corn Salad 116

Raw Veggie Picnic Salad 117

Greek Salad, The Best! 118

Sliced Tomatoes with Fresh Herb Dressing 118

Broccoli Cranberry Salad 119

Cucumber and Dill Pasta Salad 120

Grilled Vegetable Salad with Fresh Herb Vinaigrette

Prep: 30 mins **Cook:** 10 mins **Additional:** 20 mins **Total:** 1 hr **Servings:** 8 **Yield:** 8 servings

Ingredients

Vinaigrette:

- 1 shallot, minced
- 3 tablespoons red wine vinegar
- 1 tablespoon white balsamic vinegar
- 1 clove garlic, minced
- 1 tablespoon fresh lemon juice
- 1 tablespoon Dijon mustard
- 1 tablespoon chopped fresh flat-leaf parsley
- 1 tablespoon chopped fresh chives
- 1 tablespoon chopped fresh cilantro
- 1 tablespoon chopped fresh dill
- ½ cup extra-virgin olive oil, or more to taste

Vegetable Salad:

- 10 large spear (7-1/4" to 8-1/2" long)s fresh asparagus spears, trimmed to 5 inches
- 2 ears corn, husked
- 2 medium (blank)s zucchini, halved lengthwise
- 2 medium (blank)s yellow squash, halved lengthwise
- 1 bunch green onions, tops trimmed a few inches
- 1 large red bell pepper, cut lengthwise into 4 sections and seeded
- 1 large red onion, sliced thickly
- ¼ cup olive oil, or as needed
- 1 pinch salt and ground black pepper to taste

Directions

- **Step 1**
- Preheat an outdoor grill for medium-high heat and lightly oil the grate.
- **Step 2**
- Whisk shallot, red wine vinegar, white balsamic vinegar, garlic, lemon juice, Dijon mustard, parsley, chives, cilantro, and dill together in a large bowl. Slowly stream olive oil into the mixture while whisking vigorously until the oil is incorporated into a smooth and creamy dressing.
- **Step 3**

- Arrange asparagus, corn, zucchini, yellow squash, green onions, bell pepper, and red onion onto baking sheets. Brush olive oil onto all the vegetables to coat; season with salt and pepper.
- **Step 4**
- Cook vegetables directly on preheated grill, turning frequently, until slightly charred and just tender, about 5 minutes for green onions, 8 minutes for asparagus, zucchini, yellow squash, bell pepper, and red onion, and 10 minutes for corn. Remove vegetables to the baking sheets used for preparation and cool.
- **Step 5**
- Cut asparagus, green onions, zucchini, yellow squash, and red bell pepper crosswise into 1-inch pieces and put into a large bowl. Quarter red onion slices; add to bowl. Cut corn kernels from cobs; add to bowl. Let vegetables cool to room temperature.
- **Step 6**
- Drizzle vinaigrette over the vegetable mixture and toss to coat.

Cook's Note:

You may not wish to use the entire recipe of the dressing for the salad, depending on taste.

Nutrition Facts

Per Serving:

260.9 calories; protein 3.5g 7% DV; carbohydrates 16.4g 5% DV; fat 21.4g 33% DV; cholesterolmg; sodium 64.9mg 3% DV.

Healthy Garden Salad

Ingredients

8 servings 252 cals

- 5 tablespoons red wine vinegar
- 3 tablespoons grapeseed oil
- 1/3 cup chopped fresh cilantro
- 2 limes, juiced
- 1 teaspoon white sugar
- 3/4 teaspoon salt
- 2 cloves garlic, minced
- 1 (1 pound) package frozen shelled edamame (green soybeans)
- 3 cups frozen corn kernels
- 1 pint cherry tomatoes, quartered
- 4 green onions, thinly sliced
- 1 (15 ounce) can black beans, rinsed and drained

Directions

- In a large serving bowl, whisk together the red wine vinegar, grapeseed oil, cilantro, lime juice, sugar, salt and garlic. Set aside.

- Bring a large pot of lightly salted water to a boil. Add the soybeans and boil for 3 minutes. Add corn to the boiling water and continue cooking for 1 more minute. Drain very well, and pour into the bowl with the dressing. Gently mix in the cherry tomatoes, green onions and black beans. Cover and refrigerate for at least 2 hours before serving to chill and blend the flavors.

Nutrition Facts

Per Serving: 252 calories; 9.8 g fat; 33.4 g carbohydrates; 13.1 g protein; 0 mg cholesterol; 438 mg sodium.

Crispy Cucumbers and Tomatoes in Dill Dressing

Ingredients

30 m 6 servings 71 cals

- 1/4 cup cider vinegar
- 1 teaspoon white sugar
- 1/2 teaspoon salt
- 1/2 teaspoon chopped fresh dill weed
- 1/4 teaspoon ground black pepper
- 2 tablespoons vegetable oil
- 2 cucumbers, sliced
- 1 cup sliced red onion
- 2 ripe tomatoes, cut into wedges

Directions

Prep 15 m Ready In 30 m

- In a large bowl, mix the vinegar, sugar, salt, dill, pepper, and oil. Add cucumbers, onion, and tomatoes. Toss, and let stand at least 15 minutes before serving.

Nutrition Facts

Per Serving: 71 calories; 4.7 g fat; 6.7 g carbohydrates; 1 g protein; 0 mg cholesterol; 199 mg sodium.

Insalata Caprese II

Ingredients

15 m 6 servings 311 cals

- 4 large ripe tomatoes, sliced 1/4 inch thick
- 1 pound fresh mozzarella cheese, sliced 1/4 inch thick
- 1/3 cup fresh basil leaves
- 3 tablespoons extra virgin olive oil
- fine sea salt to taste

- freshly ground black pepper to taste

Directions

Prep 15 m Ready In 15 m

- On a large platter, alternate and overlap the tomato slices, mozzarella cheese slices, and basil leaves. Drizzle with olive oil. Season with sea salt and pepper.

Nutrition Facts

Per Serving: 311 calories; 23.9 g fat; 6.6 g carbohydrates; 17.9 g protein; 60 mg cholesterol; 627 mg sodium.

Cucumber Sunomono

Ingredients

1 h 15 m 5 servings 27 cals

- 2 large cucumbers, peeled
- 1/3 cup rice vinegar
- 4 teaspoons white sugar
- 1 teaspoon salt
- 1 1/2 teaspoons minced fresh ginger root

Directions

Prep 15 m Ready In 1 h 15 m

- Cut cucumbers in half lengthwise and scoop out any large seeds. Slice crosswise into very thin slices.
- In a small bowl combine vinegar, sugar, salt and ginger. Mix well. Place cucumbers inside of the bowl, stir so that cucumbers are coated with the mixture. Refrigerate the bowl of cucumbers for at least 1 hour before serving.

Nutrition Facts

Per Serving: 27 calories; 0.2 g fat; 6.2 g carbohydrates; 0.6 g protein; 0 mg cholesterol; 467 mg sodium.

Roasted Yam and Kale Salad

Ingredients

1 h 15 m 6 servings 274 cals

- 2 jewel yams, cut into 1-inch cubes
- 2 tablespoons olive oil
- salt and freshly ground black pepper to taste
- 1 tablespoon olive oil
- 1 onion, sliced
- 3 cloves garlic, minced

- 1 bunch kale, torn into bite-sized pieces
- 2 tablespoons red wine vinegar
- 1 teaspoon chopped fresh thyme

Directions

Prep 20 m Cook 20 m Ready In 1 h 15 m

- Preheat an oven to 400 degrees F (200 degrees C). Toss the yams with 2 tablespoons of olive oil in a bowl. Season to taste with salt and pepper, and arrange evenly onto a baking sheet.
- Bake in the preheated oven until the yams are tender, 20 to 25 minutes. Cool to room temperature in the refrigerator.
- Meanwhile, heat the remaining 1 tablespoon of olive oil in a large skillet over medium heat. Cook and stir the onion and garlic until the onion has caramelized to a golden brown, about 15 minutes. Stir in the kale, cooking until wilted and tender. Transfer the kale mixture to a bowl, and cool to room temperature in the refrigerator.
- Once all the ingredients have cooled, combine the yams, kale, red wine vinegar, and fresh thyme in a bowl. Season to taste with salt and pepper, and gently stir to combine.

Footnotes

- Partner Tip
- Reynolds Aluminum foil can be used to keep food moist, cook it evenly, and make clean-up easier.

Nutrition Facts

Per Serving: 274 calories; 7.5 g fat; 49.2 g carbohydrates; 5 g protein; 0 mg cholesterol; 46 mg sodium.

Tangy Cucumber and Avocado Salad

Ingredients

45 m 4 servings 186 cals

- 2 medium cucumbers, cubed
- 2 avocados, cubed
- 4 tablespoons chopped fresh cilantro
- 1 clove garlic, minced
- 2 tablespoons minced green onions (optional)
- 1/4 teaspoon salt
- black pepper to taste
- 1/4 large lemon
- 1 lime

Directions

Prep 15 m Ready In 45 m

- In a large bowl, combine cucumbers, avocados, and cilantro. Stir in garlic, onions, salt, and pepper. Squeeze lemon and lime over the top, and toss. Cover, and refrigerate at least 30 minutes.

Nutrition Facts

Per Serving: 186 calories; 14.9 g fat; 15.5 g carbohydrates; 3.1 g protein; 0 mg cholesterol; 157 mg sodium.

Tomato, Basil, and Feta Salad

Ingredients

15 m 4 servings 140 cals

- 6 roma (plum) tomatoes, diced
- 1 small cucumber - peeled, quartered lengthwise, and chopped
- 3 green onions, chopped
- 1/4 cup fresh basil leaves, cut into thin strips
- 3 tablespoons olive oil
- 2 tablespoons balsamic vinegar
- 3 tablespoons crumbled feta cheese
- salt and freshly ground black pepper to taste

Directions

Prep 15 m Ready In 15 m

- In a large bowl, toss together the tomatoes, cucumber, green onions, basil, olive oil, balsamic vinegar, and feta cheese. Season with salt and pepper.

Nutrition Facts

Per Serving: 140 calories; 11.9 g fat; 7.4 g carbohydrates; 2.4 g protein; 6 mg cholesterol; 89 mg sodium.

Mom's Cucumbers

Ingredients

5 servings 68 cals

- 3 large cucumbers
- 1 teaspoon salt
- 1/4 cup white sugar
- 1/8 cup water
- 1/4 cup distilled white vinegar
- 1/2 teaspoon celery seed
- 1/4 cup chopped onion

Directions

- Peel the cucumbers and slice wafer thin. Sprinkle with salt. Let stand 30 minutes, then squeeze cucumbers to release moisture.

- In a medium size bowl mix sugar, water, vinegar, celery seed, and onion. Add cucumbers to mixture. Mix well. Refrigerate 1 hour.

Nutrition Facts

Per Serving: 68 calories; 0.2 g fat; 17 g carbohydrates; 1.2 g protein; 0 mg cholesterol; 469 mg sodium.

Chickpea Salad with Red Onion and Tomato

Ingredients

2 h 10 m 4 servings 262 cals

- 19 ounces garbanzo beans, drained
- 2 tablespoons red onion, chopped
- 2 cloves garlic, minced
- 1 tomato, chopped
- 1/2 cup chopped parsley
- 3 tablespoons olive oil
- 1 tablespoon lemon juice
- salt and pepper to taste

Directions

Prep 10 m Ready In 2 h 10 m

- In a large bowl, combine the chickpeas, red onion, garlic, tomato, parsley, olive oil, lemon juice and salt and pepper to taste. Chill for 2 hours before serving. Taste and adjust seasoning. Serve.

Nutrition Facts

Per Serving: 262 calories; 11.8 g fat; 33.3 g carbohydrates; 7.3 g protein; 0 mg cholesterol; 404 mg sodium.

Chrissy's Sweet 'n' Sour Tomato Salad

Ingredients

30 m 6 servings 261 cals

- 7 tomatoes
- 1 small yellow onion
- 1/2 cup white sugar
- 1/2 cup distilled white vinegar
- 1/2 cup vegetable oil
- salt and pepper to taste

Directions

Prep 30 m Ready In 30 m

- Thinly slice the tomatoes. Cut the onion in half through root end, then thinly slice into half-circles. Watch Now
- In a large bowl, toss together tomatoes, onion, sugar, vinegar, oil, salt, and pepper. You may adjust the amounts of vinegar and sugar according to your taste. Serve at room temperature. Watch Now

Nutrition Facts

Per Serving: 261 calories; 18.3 g fat; 23.6 g carbohydrates; 1.3 g protein; 0 mg cholesterol; 24 mg sodium.

Broccoli-Cauliflower Salad

Ingredients

25 m 8 servings 400 cals

- 1 cup broccoli florets
- 1 cup cauliflower florets
- 2 cups hard-cooked eggs, diced (optional)
- 1 cup shredded Cheddar cheese
- 6 slices bacon
- 1 cup mayonnaise
- 1/2 cup white sugar
- 2 tablespoons white wine vinegar

Directions

Prep 10 m Cook 15 m Ready In 25 m

- Place bacon in a large, deep skillet. Cook over medium high heat until evenly brown. Crumble and set aside.
- In a medium sized salad bowl, layer in order the broccoli, cauliflower, eggs, cheese and bacon.
- Prepare the dressing by whisking together the mayonnaise, sugar and vinegar. Drizzle dressing over top and serve.

Nutrition Facts

Per Serving: 400 calories; 33 g fat; 15.5 g carbohydrates; 11.2 g protein; 177 mg cholesterol; 453 mg sodium.

Sun-Dried Tomato Basil Orzo

Ingredients

23 m 8 servings 255 cals

- 2 cups uncooked orzo pasta
- 1/2 cup chopped fresh basil leaves

- 1/3 cup chopped oil-packed sun-dried tomatoes
- 2 tablespoons olive oil
- 3/4 cup grated Parmesan cheese
- 1/2 teaspoon salt
- 1/2 teaspoon ground black pepper

Directions

Prep 15 m Cook 8 m Ready In 23 m

- Bring a large pot of lightly salted water to a boil. Add orzo and cook for 8 to 10 minutes or until al dente. Drain and set aside.
- Place basil leaves and sun-dried tomatoes in a food processor. Pulse 4 or 5 times until blended.
- In a large bowl, toss together the orzo, basil-tomato mixture, olive oil, Parmesan cheese, salt and pepper. Serve warm or chilled.

Nutrition Facts

Per Serving: 255 calories; 6.9 g fat; 38.8 g carbohydrates; 10 g protein; 7 mg cholesterol; 275 mg sodium.

Tomato, Cucumber and Red Onion Salad with Mint

Ingredients

1 h 15 m 6 servings 110 cals

- 2 large cucumbers - halved lengthwise, seeded and sliced
- 1/3 cup red wine vinegar
- 1 tablespoon white sugar
- 1 teaspoon salt
- 3 large tomatoes, seeded and coarsely chopped
- 2/3 cup coarsely chopped red onion
- 1/2 cup chopped fresh mint leaves
- 3 tablespoons olive oil
- salt and pepper to taste

Directions

Prep 15 m Ready In 1 h 15 m

- In a large bowl, toss together the cucumbers, vinegar, sugar and salt. Let stand at room temperature for an hour, stirring occasionally.
- Add tomatoes, onion, mint and oil to cucumbers and toss to blend. Season to taste with salt and pepper.

Footnotes

Partner Tip

Try using a Reynolds slow cooker liner in your slow cooker for easier cleanup.

Nutrition Facts

Per Serving: 110 calories; 7.1 g fat; 11.9 g carbohydrates; 1.7 g protein; 0 mg cholesterol; 395 mg sodium.

Fatoosh

Ingredients

30 m 6 servings 164 cals

- 2 pita breads
- 8 leaves romaine lettuce, torn into bite-size pieces
- 2 green onions, chopped
- 1 cucumber, chopped
- 3 tomatoes, cut into wedges
- 1/4 cup chopped fresh parsley
- 1 clove garlic, peeled and chopped
- 2 tablespoons sumac powder
- 1/4 cup lemon juice
- 1/4 cup olive oil
- 1 teaspoon salt
- 1/4 teaspoon ground black pepper
- 1/4 cup chopped fresh mint leaves

Directions

Prep 20 m Cook 10 m Ready In 30 m

- Preheat oven to 350 degrees F (175 degrees C).
- Toast pitas 5 to 10 minutes in the preheated oven, until crisp. Remove from heat, and break into bite size pieces.
- In a large bowl, toss together toasted pita pieces, romaine lettuce, green onions, cucumber, and tomatoes.
- In a small bowl, mix the parsley, garlic, sumac powder, lemon juice, olive oil, salt, pepper, and mint. Pour over the pita mixture, and toss just before serving.

Nutrition Facts

Per Serving: 164 calories; 9.5 g fat; 17.8 g carbohydrates; 3.2 g protein; 0 mg cholesterol; 503 mg sodium.

Greek Salad III

Ingredients

1 h 20 m 4 servings 197 cals

- 3 roma (plum) tomatoes, chopped

- 1 green bell pepper, sliced
- 1 small English cucumber, chopped
- 1 small onion, chopped
- 1/4 cup sliced black olives (optional)
- 2 ounces tomato basil feta cheese, crumbled
- 1/4 cup olive oil
- 1 teaspoon red wine vinegar
- 1 teaspoon lemon juice
- 1 clove garlic, minced
- 1/2 teaspoon dried oregano
- salt and pepper to taste

Directions

Prep 20 m Ready In 1 h 20 m

- In a salad bowl, combine the tomatoes, bell pepper, cucumber, onion and olives.
- Whisk together the oil, vinegar, lemon juice, garlic, oregano, salt and pepper. Let sit for 1 hour, occasionally stirring to blend flavors.
- Pour dressing over salad, add feta cheese and toss before serving.

Nutrition Facts

Per Serving: 197 calories; 17.7 g fat; 8 g carbohydrates; 3.3 g protein; 13 mg cholesterol; 241 mg sodium.

Owen's Mozzarella and Tomato Salad

Ingredients

30 m 4 servings 332 cals

- 4 large tomatoes
- 4 tablespoons olive oil
- ground black pepper to taste
- 10 ounces mozzarella cheese, thickly sliced
- 8 leaves fresh basil, torn into strips

Directions

Prep 10 m Ready In 30 m

- Chop tomatoes in half, then slice finely; arrange on four plates. Trickle a tablespoon of olive oil over each serving, and sprinkle with black pepper. Lay slices of cheese over tomatoes, and strips of basil over cheese. Cover with plastic wrap, and refrigerate for 30 minutes before serving.

Nutrition Facts

Per Serving: 332 calories; 25.2 g fat; 9.1 g carbohydrates; 18.8 g protein; 45 mg cholesterol; 448 mg sodium

Mexican Salad

Ingredients

1 h 15 m 7 servings 312 cals

- 1 (15 ounce) can black beans, rinsed and drained
- 1 (15 ounce) can garbanzo beans, drained
- 3 cups frozen corn kernels
- 1/2 onion, diced
- 2 jalapeno peppers, seeded and minced
- 1 red bell pepper, diced
- 3 tablespoons chopped fresh cilantro
- 1 roma (plum) tomato, diced
- 1/2 cup olive oil
- 3 tablespoons fresh lime juice
- 1/2 teaspoon honey
- 1 teaspoon ground black pepper
- salt to taste

Directions

Prep 15 m Ready In 1 h 15 m

- In a large bowl, combine the black beans, garbanzo beans, corn, onion, jalapenos, red bell pepper, cilantro, tomato, olive oil, lime juice, honey, pepper and salt. Mix well and allow to sit 1 hour before serving.

Nutrition Facts

Per Serving: 312 calories; 17 g fat; 35.1 g carbohydrates; 7.8 g protein; 0 mg cholesterol; 309 mg sodium.

Balsamic Pea Salad

Ingredients

10 m 8 servings 255 cals

- 1 (16 ounce) package frozen green peas
- 1/2 cup chopped almonds
- 1/2 cup chopped green onions
- 1/2 cup crumbled feta cheese
- 3/4 cup mayonnaise

- 2 tablespoons balsamic vinegar
- black pepper to taste

Directions

Prep 10 m Ready In 10 m

- Place peas in a colander, and run warm water over them until they are thawed. Place in a large bowl.
- Toast almonds in a skillet over medium heat. Then combine with peas.
- Stir in onions, feta cheese, and mayonnaise. Mix in balsamic vinegar, and season with pepper. Cover, and refrigerator.

Nutrition Facts

Per Serving: 255 calories; 21.6 g fat; 11 g carbohydrates; 5.8 g protein; 16 mg cholesterol; 287 mg sodium.

Couscous and Cucumber Salad

Ingredients

1 h 20 m 8 servings 142 cals

- 10 ounces uncooked couscous
- 2 tablespoons olive oil
- 1/2 cup lemon juice
- 3/4 teaspoon salt
- 1/4 teaspoon ground black pepper
- 1 cucumber, seeded and chopped
- 1/2 cup finely chopped green onions
- 1/2 cup fresh parsley, chopped
- 1/4 cup fresh basil, chopped
- 6 leaves lettuce
- 6 slices lemon

Directions

Prep 10 m Cook 10 m Ready In 1 h 20 m

- In a medium saucepan, bring 1 3/4 cup water to a boil. Stir in couscous; cover. Remove from heat; let stand, covered, 5 minutes. Cool to room temperature.
- Meanwhile, in a medium bowl combine oil, lemon juice, salt and pepper. Stir in cucumber, green onion, parsley, basil and couscous. Mix well and chill for at least 1 hour.
- Line a plate with lettuce leaves. Spoon couscous mixture over leaves and garnish with lemon wedges.

Nutrition Facts

Per Serving: 142 calories; 3.6 g fat; 24.6 g carbohydrates; 4 g protein; 0 mg cholesterol; 227 mg sodium.

Penne, Tomato, and Mozzarella Salad

Ingredients

40 m 6 servings 405 cals

- 1 (12 ounce) package penne pasta
- 1/4 cup olive oil
- 1 bunch green onions, chopped
- 1 clove garlic, minced
- 1 cup quartered cherry tomatoes
- salt and pepper to taste
- 5 ounces mozzarella cheese, diced
- 1/2 cup grated Parmesan cheese
- 4 ounces fresh basil
- 12 large black olives, halved

Directions

Prep 20 m Cook 20 m Ready In 40 m

- Cook pasta in a large pot of boiling salted water as directed on package, until just tender. Drain, and set aside.
- Heat olive oil in a small saucepan. Add green onions and cook, stirring occasionally, 2 or 3 minutes. Stir in garlic, and cook for 2 minutes. Add pasta, tomatoes, salt, and pepper. Cook over low heat to warm through. Stir in mozzarella and Parmesan cheese. Coarsely tear basil leaves in halves or thirds; add to pasta with olives, and serve immediately.

Nutrition Facts

Per Serving: 405 calories; 17.2 g fat; 47.5 g carbohydrates; 17.5 g protein; 21 mg cholesterol; 337 mg sodium.

Black Bean, Corn, and Tomato Salad with Feta Cheese

Ingredients

9 h 12 servings 285 cals

- 1 (14 ounce) can black beans, drained and rinsed
- 2 fresh tomatoes, chopped
- 1 large green bell pepper, chopped

- 1 cup fresh sweet white corn, cut from the cob
- 1 bunch green onions, sliced
- 1 jicama, peeled and minced
- 1 fresh jalapeno pepper, minced
- 1 (8 ounce) package crumbled feta cheese
- 1 clove garlic
- 1 pinch sea salt
- 1/4 cup fresh lime juice
- 1 teaspoon Dijon mustard
- 1/4 teaspoon fresh-ground black pepper
- 1 cup olive oil

Directions

Prep 1 h Ready In 9 h

- Place the beans, tomato, bell pepper, corn, onion, jicama, jalapeno pepper, and feta cheese in a large salad bowl.
- Mash the garlic and salt together with a mortar and pestle. Whisk together the mashed garlic, lime juice, mustard, and pepper in a small bowl. Add the oil in a slow, steady stream while whisking. Continue whisking until smooth. Drizzle the dressing over the salad and toss to coat. Chill overnight.

Nutrition Facts

Per Serving: 285 calories; 22.4 g fat; 16.8 g carbohydrates; 6.1 g protein; 17 mg cholesterol; 384 mg sodium.

Fresh Tomato Salad

Ingredients

30 m 7 servings 39 cals

- 5 tomatoes, diced
- 1 onion, chopped
- 1 cucumber, sliced
- 1 green bell pepper, chopped
- 1/2 cup chopped fresh basil
- 1/2 cup chopped parsley
- 2 tablespoons crushed garlic
- salt and pepper to taste
- 2 tablespoons white wine vinegar

Directions

Prep 15 m Ready In 30 m

- In a large bowl, combine the tomato, onion, cucumber, bell pepper, basil, parsley, garlic and vinegar. Toss and add salt and pepper to taste. Chill and serve.

Nutrition Facts

Per Serving: 39 calories; 0.4 g fat; 8.6 g carbohydrates; 1.8 g protein; 0 mg cholesterol; 10 mg sodium.

Carrot Salad

Ingredients

15 m 8 servings 58 cals

- 4 carrots, shredded
- 1 apple - peeled, cored and shredded
- 1 tablespoon lemon juice
- 2 tablespoons honey
- 1/4 cup blanched slivered almonds
- salt and pepper to taste

Directions

Prep 15 m Ready In 15 m

- In a bowl, combine the carrots, apple, lemon juice, honey, almonds, salt and pepper. Toss and chill before serving.

Nutrition Facts

Per Serving: 58 calories; 1.8 g fat; 10.5 g carbohydrates; 1.1 g protein; 0 mg cholesterol; 22 mg sodium.

Sesame Broccoli Salad

Ingredients

25 m 8 servings 78 cals

- 2 tablespoons sesame seeds
- 1 1/2 pounds fresh broccoli, cut into bite size pieces
- 2 tablespoons rice vinegar
- 2 tablespoons soy sauce
- 2 tablespoons sesame oil
- 2 teaspoons white sugar

Directions

Prep 15 m Cook 10 m Ready In 25 m

- Preheat oven to 375 degrees F (190 degrees C). Toast sesame seeds for 3 to 5 minutes, or until the seeds begin to turn golden brown. Set aside.

- Bring a large pot of water to a boil. Cook broccoli in boiling water for 3 to 5 minutes, or until desired tenderness. Drain, and transfer to a large bowl.
- In a small bowl, whisk together the vinegar, soy sauce, sesame oil, sugar, and sesame seeds. Pour over broccoli, and toss to coat.

Nutrition Facts

Per Serving: 78 calories; 4.8 g fat; 7.5 g carbohydrates; 3.1 g protein; 0 mg cholesterol; 254 mg sodium.

Celery Salad

Ingredients

40 m 2 servings 150 cals

- 3/4 cup sliced celery
- 1/3 cup dried sweet cherries
- 1/3 cup frozen green peas, thawed
- 3 tablespoons chopped fresh parsley
- 1 tablespoon chopped pecans, toasted
- 1 1/2 tablespoons fat-free mayonnaise
- 1 1/2 tablespoons plain low-fat yogurt
- 1 1/2 teaspoons fresh lemon juice
- 1/8 teaspoon salt
- 1/8 teaspoon ground black pepper

Directions

Prep 10 m Ready In 40 m

- In a medium bowl, combine the celery, cherries, peas, parsley and pecans. Stir in the mayonnaise, yogurt and lemon juice. Season with salt and pepper. Chill before serving.

Nutrition Facts

Per Serving: 150 calories; 3 g fat; 26.5 g carbohydrates; 4.1 g protein; < 1 mg cholesterol; 304 mg sodium.

Hungarian Cucumber Salad

Ingredients

15 m 6 servings 98 cals

- 2 large seedless English cucumbers, sliced thin
- 1 extra large onions, sliced thin
- 1/4 cup chopped fresh dill
- 3 tablespoons white vinegar
- 3 tablespoons vegetable oil

- 1 teaspoon salt, or to taste
- 1/2 teaspoon ground black pepper, or to taste

Directions

Prep 15 m Ready In 15 m

- Lightly toss cucumber slices, onion slices, and chopped dill together in a large bowl.
- Pour vinegar over cucumber mixture; toss to coat.
- Pour oil over cucumber mixture; toss to coat.
- Season with salt and black pepper.

Footnotes

- Cook's Note:
- The reason you add the vinegar first and then the oil is because if the cukes get oil on them first the vinegar will not be able to soak in properly. This salad will also have some liquid that comes out of the onion and cucumber. This is a good thing! Do not pour it out.

Nutrition Facts

Per Serving: 98 calories; 7 g fat; 8.9 g carbohydrates; 1.3 g protein; 0 mg cholesterol; 393 mg sodium.

Raw Vegetable Salad

Ingredients

25 m 18 servings 283 cals

- 6 slices bacon
- 3 cups chopped broccoli
- 3 cups chopped cauliflower
- 3 cups chopped celery
- 1 (10 ounce) package frozen green peas, thawed
- 1 cup sweetened dried cranberries (such as Craisins®)
- 1 1/2 cups mayonnaise
- 1/4 cup Parmesan cheese
- 1/4 cup white sugar
- 2 tablespoons grated onion
- 1 tablespoon white wine vinegar
- 1 teaspoon salt
- 1 cup Spanish peanuts

Directions

Prep 15 m Cook 10 m Ready In 25 m

- Place bacon in a large deep skillet. Cook over medium-high heat until evenly brown, 10 to 15 minutes. Drain bacon on a paper towel-lined plate; crumble.

- Mix broccoli, cauliflower, celery, peas, and cranberries in a large bowl.
- Whisk mayonnaise, Parmesan cheese, sugar, onion, vinegar, and salt together in a bowl. Pour dressing over the salad; add nuts and bacon and toss well.

Nutrition Facts

Per Serving: 283 calories; 23.3 g fat; 15 g carbohydrates; 5.5 g protein; 14 mg cholesterol; 373 mg sodium.

Tomato and Avocado Salad

Ingredients

15 m 4 servings 236 cals

- 1 teaspoon Dijon mustard
- 1/4 cup extra-virgin olive oil
- 1/2 cup balsamic vinegar
- 1 pinch ground black pepper
- 1 avocado - peeled, pitted and sliced
- 2 small tomatoes, each cut into 8 wedges

Directions

Prep 15 m Ready In 15 m

- In a small bowl, whisk together the mustard, olive oil, balsamic vinegar and pepper. Arrange the slices of avocado and tomato alternately like the spokes of a wheel on one big serving plate, or individual plates. Drizzle lightly with the dressing, and serve immediately.

Nutrition Facts

Per Serving: 236 calories; 21.5 g fat; 11.1 g carbohydrates; 1.5 g protein; 0 mg cholesterol; 45 mg sodium.

Tofu Salad

Ingredients

1 h 20 m 4 servings 145 cals

- 1 tablespoon sweet chili sauce
- 1/2 teaspoon grated fresh ginger root
- 2 cloves garlic, crushed
- 1 tablespoon dark soy sauce
- 1 tablespoon sesame oil
- 1/2 (16 ounce) package extra-firm tofu, drained and diced
- 1 cup snow peas, trimmed
- 2 small carrots, grated

- 1 cup finely shredded red cabbage
- 2 tablespoons chopped peanuts

Directions

Prep 15 m Cook 2 m Ready In 1 h 20 m

- In a large bowl, mix the chili sauce, ginger, garlic, soy sauce, and sesame oil. Place tofu in the mixture, and marinate 1 hour in the refrigerator.
- Bring a pot of water to a boil. Immerse the snow peas in the boiling water for 1 to 2 minutes, then immerse in a a bowl of cold water. Drain, and set aside.
- Toss the peas, carrots, cabbage, and peanuts with the tofu and marinade to serve.

Nutrition Facts

Per Serving: 145 calories; 9.1 g fat; 10.1 g carbohydrates; 8.2 g protein; 0 mg cholesterol; 295 mg sodium.

Chinese-Style Broccoli Salad

Ingredients

4 servings 188 cals

- 2 heads fresh broccoli
- 2 tablespoons vegetable oil
- 1 tablespoon salt
- 2 tablespoons light soy sauce
- 2 tablespoons distilled white vinegar
- 2 tablespoons sesame oil
- 1/4 teaspoon salt
- 1 tablespoon white sugar

Directions

- Separate broccoli into bite-sized florets. Peel tough skin off stem and quarter it into 2 inch pieces cut slantwise.
- Bring 2 1/2 quarts water, 2 tablespoons oil and 1 tablespoon salt to boil. Add broccoli and boil quickly for 1 minute; plunge into cold water to set color; drain and place on platter or in a bowl.
- In a small bowl combine soy sauce, vinegar, sesame oil, 1/4 teaspoon salt and sugar. Pour mixture over broccoli, toss. This salad can be served hot or cold, your choice!

Nutrition Facts

Per Serving: 188 calories; 14.2 g fat; 13.8 g carbohydrates; 4.6 g protein; 0 mg cholesterol; 2205 mg sodium.

Marinated Beet Salad

Ingredients

4 h 20 m 4 servings 89 cals

- 1 (16 ounce) can whole beets
- 1/4 cup white sugar
- 1 teaspoon prepared mustard
- 1/4 cup white wine vinegar
- 1/4 cup diced red onion

Directions

Prep 10 m Cook 10 m Ready In 4 h 20 m

- Drain beets, reserving 1/4 cup liquid, and slice into 1/4 to 1/2 inch slivers. Add onions and toss.
- In a saucepan over medium heat, cook the sugar, mustard and reserved 1/4 cup liquid until dissolved. Add vinegar and bring to boil; remove from heat and allow to cool.
- Pour over the beet slices and onions, toss and refrigerate for 4 to 6 hours. Remove from refrigerator and serve at room temperature.

Nutrition Facts

Per Serving: 89 calories; 0.2 g fat; 21.7 g carbohydrates; 1.2 g protein; 0 mg cholesterol; 236 mg sodium.

Tomato-Mint Quinoa Salad

Ingredients

1 h 55 m 4 servings 346 cals

- 2 1/2 cups water
- 1 1/4 cups quinoa
- 1/3 cup raisins
- 1 pinch salt
- 2 medium tomatoes, diced
- 1 medium onion, minced
- 10 radishes, quartered
- 1/2 cucumber, diced
- 2 tablespoons sliced almonds, toasted
- 1/4 cup chopped fresh mint
- 2 tablespoons chopped fresh parsley
- 1 teaspoon ground cumin
- 1/4 cup lime juice
- 2 tablespoons sesame oil
- salt to taste

Directions

Prep 40 m Cook 15 m Ready In 1 h 55 m

- Bring water to boil in a small saucepan. Pour in quinoa, raisins, and a pinch of salt. Cover, and let simmer for 12 to 15 minutes, then remove from heat, and allow to cool to room temperature.
- Toss together the tomatoes, onion, radish, cucumber, and almonds in a large bowl. Stir in the cooled quinoa, then season with mint, parsley, cumin, lime juice, sesame oil, and salt. Chill 1 to 2 hours before serving.

Nutrition Facts

Per Serving: 346 calories; 11.8 g fat; 53.3 g carbohydrates; 9.5 g protein; 0 mg cholesterol; 178 mg sodium.

Bacon Pea Salad

Ingredients

50 m 8 servings 281 cals

- 4 slices bacon
- 3/4 cup mayonnaise
- 1 tablespoon honey
- 1 tablespoon white sugar
- salt and ground black pepper to taste
- 1 (20 ounce) package fresh green peas
- 2 stalks celery, chopped
- 1/2 cup cubed Cheddar cheese
- 1/3 cup chopped onion

Directions

Prep 10 m Cook 10 m Ready In 50 m

- Place bacon in a large skillet and cook over medium-high heat, turning occasionally, until evenly browned, about 10 minutes. Drain bacon slices on paper towels and crumble. Reserve 1 tablespoon bacon grease.
- Whisk mayonnaise, reserved bacon grease, honey, sugar, salt, and black pepper together in a bowl until dressing is smooth.
- Mix bacon, peas, celery, Cheddar cheese, and onion together in a bowl. Drizzle dressing over salad and toss to coat. Refrigerate until chilled, about 30 minutes.

Footnotes

- Partner Tip
- Reynolds Aluminum foil can be used to keep food moist, cook it evenly, and make clean-up easier.

Nutrition Facts

Per Serving: 281 calories; 21.3 g fat; 15.6 g carbohydrates; 7.9 g protein; 21 mg cholesterol; 304 mg sodium.

Cucumber Salad with Dill Vinaigrette

Prep: 20 mins **Total:** 20 mins **Servings:** 4 **Yield:** 4 servings

Ingredients

- 1 pint grape tomatoes, halved
- 3 medium (blank)s cucumbers - peeled, seeded, and chopped
- 1 red onion, chopped
- 2 medium (blank)s yellow bell peppers, chopped
- ¼ cup cider vinegar
- ¼ cup olive oil
- 1 (4 ounce) jar capers, drained
- 2 teaspoons dried dill

Directions

- **Step 1**
  Mix tomatoes, cucumbers, red onion, and yellow bell peppers in a bowl; add vinegar, olive oil, capers, and dill. Toss to evenly coat vegetables with dressing.

Nutrition Facts

Per Serving:

193.3 calories; protein 3.2g 6% DV; carbohydrates 15.4g 5% DV; fat 14.7g 23% DV; cholesterolmg; sodium 855.6mg 34% DV.

Easy Cherry Tomato Corn Salad

Prep: 20 mins **Total:** 20 mins **Servings:** 6 **Yield:** 6 servings

Ingredients

- ¼ cup minced fresh basil
- 3 tablespoons olive oil
- 2 teaspoons lime juice
- 1 teaspoon white sugar
- ½ teaspoon salt
- ¼ teaspoon ground black pepper
- 2 cups frozen corn, thawed
- 2 cups cherry tomatoes, halved
- 1 cup peeled, seeded, and chopped cucumber
- 1 jalapeno pepper, seeded and chopped
- 2 eaches shallots, minced

Directions

- **Step 1**

  Combine basil, olive oil, lime juice, sugar, salt, and pepper in a jar and screw on the lid; shake until dressing is completely blended.

- **Step 2**

  Stir corn, tomatoes, cucumber, jalapeno, and shallots together in a bowl. Drizzle dressing over corn mixture and toss to coat. Refrigerate until serving.

Nutrition Facts

Per Serving:

138 calories; protein 2.7g 6% DV; carbohydrates 18.4g 6% DV; fat 7.4g 11% DV; cholesterolmg; sodium 202.6mg 8% DV.

Broccoli Cauliflower Pepita Salad

Prep: 15 mins **Additional:** 1 hr **Total:** 1 hr 15 mins **Servings:** 10 **Yield:** 10 servings

Ingredients

- 3 cups coarsely diced broccoli
- 3 cups coarsely diced cauliflower
- 1 red bell pepper, diced
- ½ cup diced onion
- ½ cup shelled roasted pumpkin seeds (pepitas)
- ½ cup light mayonnaise
- ½ cup plain nonfat Greek yogurt
- 2 tablespoons red wine vinegar
- 2 tablespoons coconut palm sugar
- 1 teaspoon Dijon mustard
- ½ teaspoon salt

Directions

- **Step 1**

  Mix broccoli, cauliflower, red bell pepper, onion, and pumpkin seeds in a large bowl.

- **Step 2**

  Whisk mayonnaise, yogurt, red wine vinegar, palm sugar, Dijon mustard, and salt together in a separate bowl; drizzle over the broccoli mixture and toss to coat.

- **Step 3**

  Cover bowl with plastic wrap and refrigerate 1 to 2 hours before serving.

Nutrition Facts

Per Serving:

125.1 calories; protein 3.9g 8% DV; carbohydrates 10.4g 3% DV; fat 8.3g 13% DV; cholesterol 6.4mg 2% DV; sodium 250.6mg 10% DV.

Red Potato, Asparagus, and Artichoke Salad

Prep: 25 mins **Cook:** 35 mins **Additional:** 1 hr **Total:** 2 hrs **Servings:** 8 **Yield:** 8 servings

Ingredients

- 18 small red potatoes
- 3 pounds fresh asparagus, trimmed
- 2 (14 ounce) cans artichoke hearts, drained and quartered
- 3 tablespoons Dijon mustard
- ¼ cup fresh lemon juice
- ¾ cup olive oil
- 1 pinch salt and ground black pepper to taste
- ¼ teaspoon cayenne pepper, or to taste
- 5 tablespoons minced fresh chives

Directions

- **Step 1**

  Place the potatoes into a large pot and cover with salted water. Bring to a boil over high heat, then reduce heat to medium-low, cover, and simmer until tender, about 20 minutes. Drain and allow to steam dry for a minute or two. Allow to cool completely before cutting into bite-size cubes. Transfer to a large bowl

- **Step 2**

  Bring a large pot of salted water to a boil over high heat. Add the asparagus spears, and cook until tender, about 3 minutes depending on size. Drain and immediately plunge into cold water to stop cooking. Cut the asparagus spears into 1 inch pieces. Place in the bowl with the potatoes. Stir in the artichokes, breaking them apart slightly as you put them in the bowl.

- **Step 3**

  Combine the mustard and lemon juice in a bowl; whisk the oil gradually into the mustard and lemon juice until smooth. Season with salt, pepper, and cayenne pepper to taste. Drizzle over the vegetables; toss to coat. Sprinkle with chives to serve.

Nutrition Facts

Per Serving:

552.8 calories; protein 12.4g 25% DV; carbohydrates 84g 27% DV; fat 21g 32% DV; cholesterolmg; sodium 540.7mg 22% DV.

Vegan Black Bean and Sweet Potato Salad

Prep: 15 mins **Cook:** 25 mins **Total:** 40 mins **Servings:** 4 **Yield:** 4 servings

Ingredients

- 1 pound sweet potatoes, peeled and cut into 3/4-inch cubes
- 3 tablespoons olive oil, divided
- ½ teaspoon ground cumin, or more to taste
- ¼ teaspoon red pepper flakes
- 1 pinch coarse salt and ground black pepper to taste
- 2 tablespoons freshly squeezed lime juice
- 1 (14.5 ounce) can black beans, rinsed and drained
- ½ red onion, finely chopped
- ½ cup chopped fresh cilantro

Directions

- **Step 1**

  Preheat oven to 450 degrees F (230 degrees C).

- **Step 2**

  Spread sweet potatoes onto a rimmed baking sheet. Drizzle 1 tablespoon olive oil over sweet potatoes; season with cumin, red pepper flakes, salt, and pepper. Toss sweet potatoes until evenly coated.

- **Step 3**

  Roast on the lower rack of the preheated oven, stirring halfway through, until sweet potatoes are tender, 25 to 35 minutes.

- **Step 4**

  Whisk remaining 2 tablespoons olive oil and lime juice together in a large bowl; season with salt and pepper. Add sweet potatoes, black beans, onion, and cilantro; gently toss to coat.

Nutrition Facts

Per Serving:

291.1 calories; protein 8.4g 17% DV; carbohydrates 42.2g 14% DV; fat 10.6g 16% DV; cholesterolmg; sodium 461.8mg 19% DV.

My Favorite Beet Salad

Prep: 30 mins **Cook:** 1 hr **Total:** 1 hr 30 mins **Servings:** 8 **Yield:** 8 servings

Ingredients

- 6 large beets, trimmed

- ¼ cup extra virgin olive oil
- 1 pinch salt and ground black pepper to taste
- 1 (8 ounce) package baby spinach leaves
- 2 medium whole (2-3/5" dia) (blank)s tomatoes, cut into bite-sized pieces
- 2 medium (blank)s avocados - peeled, pitted, and cut into bite-sized pieces
- ½ red onion, chopped, or to taste
- 1 (4 ounce) container crumbled feta cheese
- ½ cup balsamic vinegar
- ½ cup extra-virgin olive oil
- 1 tablespoon Dijon mustard, or more to taste

Directions

- **Step 1**

  Preheat oven to 375 degrees F (190 degrees C).

- **Step 2**

  Place the beets into a large bowl, and drizzle with 1/4 cup olive oil, salt, and black pepper. Lay out 2 large squares of aluminum foil on a work surface, and place 3 beets onto the center of each sheet. Fold the aluminum foil into 2 envelopes, sealing the beets into the packets; place the packets into a baking dish.

- **Step 3**

  Bake in the preheated oven until tender, 1 to 1 1/2 hours. Check for tenderness after 1 hour by piercing a beet with a fork. Open the foil, and allow the beets to cool until they can be handled; peel, and slice.

- **Step 4**

  Lay out the spinach leaves on an attractive oblong-shaped serving platter. Sprinkle pieces of tomato and avocado over the spinach leaves, and top with chopped red onion. Lay the sliced warm beets over the salad, and top with crumbled feta cheese.

- **Step 5**

  Whisk together balsamic vinegar, 1/2 cup of olive oil, and Dijon mustard until smooth; pour over the salad to serve.

Nutrition Facts

Per Serving:

413.1 calories; protein 7.2g 14% DV; carbohydrates 28.2g 9% DV; fat 31.9g 49% DV; cholesterol 12.6mg 4% DV; sodium 400.3mg 16% DV.

Persian-Style Tomato Avocado Salad

Prep: 20 mins **Total:** 20 mins **Servings:** 4 **Yield:** 4 servings

Ingredients

- 4 eaches ripe tomatoes, diced

- 2 medium (blank)s Hass avocados, diced
- 1 clove garlic, minced
- 3 tablespoons chopped red onion
- 6 sprigs cilantro, chopped
- 2 tablespoons fresh lime juice
- 1 pinch salt and ground black pepper to taste
- 1 lime, sliced into thin rounds

Directions

- **Step 1**

  Combine the tomatoes, avocados, garlic, onion, and cilantro in a large bowl. Sprinkle with lime juice, and season with salt and pepper. Garnish salad with thin lime slices.

Nutrition Facts

Per Serving:

197.6 calories; protein 3.6g 7% DV; carbohydrates 17.3g 6% DV; fat 15.1g 23% DV; cholesterolmg; sodium 16.9mg 1% DV.

Lemon Pea Salad

Prep: 10 mins **Total:** 10 mins **Servings:** 1 **Yield:** 1 servings

Ingredients

- 1 cup raw peas
- ½ lemon, juiced
- 1 pinch salt and ground black pepper to taste

Directions

- **Step 1**

  Mix peas, lemon juice, salt, and pepper together in a bowl.

Nutrition Facts

Per Serving:

46.8 calories; protein 2.8g 6% DV; carbohydrates 9.3g 3% DV; fat 0.2g; cholesterolmg; sodium 159.2mg 6% DV.

Marinated Cucumber, Onion, and Tomato Salad

Prep: 15 mins **Additional:** 2 hrs **Total:** 2 hrs 15 mins **Servings:** 6 **Yield:** 6 servings

Ingredients

- 1 cup water
- ½ cup distilled white vinegar
- ¼ cup vegetable oil

- ¼ cup sugar
- 2 teaspoons salt
- 1 tablespoon fresh, coarsely ground black pepper
- 3 medium (blank)s cucumbers, peeled and sliced 1/4-inch thick
- 3 eaches tomatoes, cut into wedges
- 1 onion, sliced and separated into rings

Directions

- **Step 1**

  Whisk water, vinegar, oil, sugar, salt, and pepper together in a large bowl until smooth; add cucumbers, tomatoes, and onion and stir to coat.

- **Step 2**

  Cover bowl with plastic wrap; refrigerate at least 2 hours.

Nutrition Facts

Per Serving:

156.2 calories; protein 1.8g 4% DV; carbohydrates 18g 6% DV; fat 9.5g 15% DV; cholesterolmg; sodium 784mg 31% DV.

Old Fashioned Potato Salad

Prep: 45 mins **Cook:** 15 mins **Total:** 1 hr **Servings:** 8 **Yield:** 8 servings

Ingredients

- 5 medium (2-1/4" to 3" dia, raw)s potatoes
- 3 large eggs eggs
- 1 cup chopped celery
- ½ cup chopped onion
- ½ cup sweet pickle relish
- ¼ teaspoon garlic salt
- ¼ teaspoon celery salt
- 1 tablespoon prepared mustard
- ground black pepper to taste
- ¼ cup mayonnaise

Directions

- **Step 1**

  Bring a large pot of salted water to a boil. Add potatoes and cook until tender but still firm, about 15 minutes. Drain, cool, peel and chop.

- **Step 2**

  Place eggs in a saucepan and cover with cold water. Bring water to a boil; cover, remove from heat, and let eggs stand in hot water for 10 to 12 minutes. Remove from hot water, cool, peel and chop.

- **Step 3**

  In a large bowl, combine the potatoes, eggs, celery, onion, relish, garlic salt, celery salt, mustard, pepper and mayonnaise. Mix together well and refrigerate until chilled.

Nutrition Facts

Per Serving:

206.4 calories; protein 5.5g 11% DV; carbohydrates 30.5g 10% DV; fat 7.6g 12% DV; cholesterol 72.4mg 24% DV; sodium 334.7mg 13% DV.

Dad's Creamy Cucumber Salad

Prep: 10 mins **Additional:** 3 hrs **Total:** 3 hrs 10 mins **Servings:** 8 **Yield:** 8 servings

Ingredients

- 2 large cucumbers, peeled and thinly sliced
- 1 sweet onion, thinly sliced
- 1 tablespoon sea salt
- 1 ½ cups mayonnaise, or more to taste
- 2 tablespoons vinegar
- 1 tablespoon white sugar
- 1 teaspoon dried dill weed
- 1 teaspoon garlic powder
- 1 teaspoon ground black pepper

Directions

- **Step 1**

  Mix cucumbers, sweet onion, and sea salt together in a bowl. Cover bowl with plastic wrap and let sit for 30 minutes.

- **Step 2**

  Turn cucumber mixture into a colander set over a bowl or in a sink; let drain, stirring occasionally, until most of the liquid has drained, about 30 minutes more. Transfer drained cucumber mixture to a large bowl.

- **Step 3**

  Stir mayonnaise, vinegar, sugar, dill, garlic powder, and black pepper together in a bowl with a whisk until smooth; pour over the cucumber mixture and stir to coat vegetables with the dressing.

- **Step 4**

  Cover bowl with plastic wrap and refrigerate at least 2 hours.

Cook's Note:

You can add some more mayonnaise if the sauce is too runny for your liking.

Nutrition Facts
Per Serving:

320.3 calories; protein 1.1g 2% DV; carbohydrates 6.9g 2% DV; fat 32.9g 51% DV; cholesterol 15.7mg 5% DV; sodium 896.9mg 36% DV.

Fresh Broccoli Salad

Prep: 15 mins **Cook:** 15 mins **Total:** 30 mins **Servings:** 9 **Yield:** 8 to 10 servings

Ingredients

- 2 heads fresh broccoli
- 1 red onion
- ½ pound bacon
- ¾ cup raisins
- ¾ cup sliced almonds
- 1 cup mayonnaise
- ½ cup white sugar
- 2 tablespoons white wine vinegar

Directions

- **Step 1**

  Place bacon in a deep skillet and cook over medium high heat until evenly brown. Cool and crumble.
- **Step 2**

  Cut the broccoli into bite-size pieces and cut the onion into thin bite-size slices. Combine with the bacon, raisins, your favorite nuts and mix well.
- **Step 3**

  To prepare the dressing, mix the mayonnaise, sugar and vinegar together until smooth. Stir into the salad, let chill and serve.

Nutrition Facts

Per Serving:

373.8 calories; protein 7.3g 15% DV; carbohydrates 28.5g 9% DV; fat 27.2g 42% DV; cholesterol 18.3mg 6% DV; sodium 352.9mg 14% DV.

Greek Zoodle Salad

Prep: 15 mins **Additional:** 10 mins **Total:** 25 mins **Servings:** 4 **Yield:** 4 side salads

Ingredients

- 2 medium (blank)s zucchini
- ¼ English cucumber, chopped
- 10 eaches cherry tomatoes, halved, or more to taste
- 10 eaches pitted kalamata olives, halved, or more to taste
- ¼ cup thinly sliced red onion

- 2 ounces crumbled reduced-fat feta cheese
- 2 tablespoons extra-virgin olive oil
- 2 tablespoons fresh lemon juice
- 1 teaspoon dried oregano
- 1 pinch salt and ground black pepper to taste

Directions

- **Step 1**

  Cut zucchini into noodle-shaped strands using a spiralizing tool. Place "zoodles" in a large bowl and top with cucumber, tomatoes, olives, red onion, and feta cheese.

- **Step 2**

  Whisk olive oil, lemon juice, oregano, salt, and pepper together in a bowl until dressing is smooth; pour over "zoodle" mixture and toss to coat. Marinate salad in refrigerator for 10 to 15 minutes.

Cook's Note:

You may wish to cut noodles in half to make them more manageable. After putting zucchini through spirilizer, pile on top of a cutting board and cut down center of pile with a large knife. You can also spiral cut cucumber instead of chopping.

Nutrition Facts

Per Serving:

146.6 calories; protein 5g 10% DV; carbohydrates 9.1g 3% DV; fat 11.1g 17% DV; cholesterol 5mg 2% DV; sodium 391.4mg 16% DV.

Pittsburgh Football Sunday Pasta Salad

Prep: 30 mins **Cook:** 15 mins **Total:** 45 mins **Servings:** 6 **Yield:** 6 servings

Ingredients

- 1 ½ pounds uncooked penne pasta
- ⅓ cup light mayonnaise
- 1 (8 ounce) bottle Italian-style salad dressing
- ¼ teaspoon Italian seasoning, or to taste
- ¼ teaspoon garlic powder, or to taste
- ¼ teaspoon cayenne pepper, or to taste
- 1 pinch salt and ground black pepper to taste
- ½ (12 ounce) package broccoli coleslaw mix
- 2 plum tomato (blank)s Roma tomatoes, diced
- 1 cucumber, diced
- 1 (3 ounce) can tuna, drained
- ¼ cup shredded Cheddar cheese
- ¼ cup shredded Monterey Jack cheese

- 2 eaches green onions, chopped

Directions

- **Step 1**

  Fill a large pot with lightly salted water and bring to a rolling boil over high heat. Once the water is boiling, stir in the penne, and return to a boil. Cook the pasta uncovered, stirring occasionally, until the pasta has cooked through, but is still firm to the bite, about 11 minutes. Drain well in a colander set in the sink. Rinse with cold water to stop the cooking process.

- **Step 2**

  Combine the mayonnaise, salad dressing, Italian seasoning, garlic powder, cayenne pepper, salt, and pepper in a blender; blend until completely mixed.

- **Step 3**

  Place the coleslaw mix, tomatoes, cucumber, tuna, Cheddar cheese, Monterey Jack cheese, green onions, and the cooked pasta in a large bowl; pour mayonnaise mixture into the bowl; toss to coat. Serve cold.

Nutrition Facts

Per Serving:

595.6 calories; protein 21.9g 44% DV; carbohydrates 93.3g 30% DV; fat 16.4g 25% DV; cholesterol 13.4mg 5% DV; sodium 789.2mg 32% DV.

Grilled Cheese and Veggie Sandwich

Prep: 15 mins **Cook:** 10 mins **Total:** 25 mins **Servings:** 4 **Yield:** 4 sandwiches

Ingredients

- 1 ½ cups coleslaw mix
- ½ cup bean sprouts
- 8 thick slices (3/4 inch thick) sourdough bread
- 3 tablespoons margarine, softened
- 3 tablespoons honey mustard
- 6 ounces sliced Havarti cheese

Directions

- **Step 1**

  In a medium bowl, toss together the coleslaw mix and bean sprouts.

- **Step 2**

  Spread one side of each bread slice with margarine. Spread opposite side of 4 slices with honey mustard. Layer the honey mustard side of the 4 bread slices with the coleslaw mixture and cheese. Top with remaining 4 bread slices, margarine side out.

- **Step 3**

In a large skillet over medium heat, cook the sandwiches about 2 minutes on each side, until the cheese has melted and the bread is golden brown.

Nutrition Facts

Per Serving:

506.8 calories; protein 18.5g 37% DV; carbohydrates 49.5g 16% DV; fat 27.5g 42% DV; cholesterol 55.5mg 19% DV; sodium 1008.2mg 40% DV.

Thai Chicken Slaw Burgers

Prep: 15 mins **Cook:** 15 mins **Total:** 30 mins **Servings:** 8 **Yield:** 8 servings

Ingredients

- 8 roll (blank)s hamburger buns, split
- 2 tablespoons butter
- ½ onion, chopped
- 2 tablespoons tomato paste
- 2 cloves garlic, minced
- 3 tablespoons Thai sweet chili sauce, or more to taste
- 1 tablespoon Worcestershire sauce
- 1 teaspoon white sugar
- 2 pounds boneless, skinless chicken breast, or more to taste, cut in bite-size pieces
- 2 tablespoons olive oil
- 3 tablespoons sweet pickle relish
- 3 tablespoons lemon juice
- 2 tablespoons honey
- 2 cups coleslaw mix

Directions

- **Step 1**

  Set oven rack about 6 inches from the heat source and preheat the oven's broiler. Arrange hamburger buns, cut-sides facing up, in a single layer on a baking sheet.

- **Step 2**

  Toast buns under the preheated broiler until toasted, 30 to 60 seconds.

- **Step 3**

  Melt butter in a large skillet over medium heat. Cook and stir onion, tomato paste, and garlic in hot butter until onion is softened, about 5 minutes. Stir chili sauce, Worcestershire sauce, and sugar into onion mixture.

- **Step 4**

  Stir chicken and olive oil into the skillet; cook and stir until chicken is no longer pink in the center, 5 to 10 minutes.

- **Step 5**

  Whisk relish, lemon juice, and honey together in a large bowl; add coleslaw blend and toss to coat.

- **Step 6**

  Spoon chicken mixture into toasted buns and top with coleslaw.

Cook's Note:

You can substitute 1/2 teaspoon stevia sugar substitute (such as Truvia(R)) for the 1 teaspoon sugar, if desired.

Nutrition Facts

Per Serving:

379 calories; protein 29.7g 59% DV; carbohydrates 36g 12% DV; fat 12.6g 19% DV; cholesterol 78.2mg 26% DV; sodium 488.3mg 20% DV.

Corn Salad with Creamy Italian Dressing

Prep: 20 mins **Cook:** 15 mins **Additional:** 8 hrs **Total:** 8 hrs 35 mins **Servings:** 6 **Yield:** 6 servings

Ingredients

Dressing:

- ½ cup mayonnaise
- ¼ cup red wine vinegar
- ¼ cup olive oil
- 1 clove garlic, crushed
- 2 teaspoons water
- ½ teaspoon freshly ground black pepper
- ½ teaspoon white sugar
- ¼ teaspoon salt
- ¼ teaspoon Italian seasoning
- 1 pinch cayenne pepper, or more to taste
- 1 tablespoon olive oil
- 1 (16 ounce) package frozen sweet corn, thawed
- 1 cup diced roasted red peppers
- 1 pinch salt and ground black pepper to taste
- 5 leaf (blank)s fresh basil leaves, thinly sliced, or more to taste
- 1 pinch cayenne pepper, or to taste

Directions

- **Step 1**

  Whisk mayonnaise, vinegar, 1/4 cup olive oil, garlic, water, 1/2 teaspoon black pepper, sugar, 1/4 teaspoon salt, Italian seasoning, and a pinch cayenne pepper together in a bowl until dressing is thick and creamy. Cover dressing with plastic wrap and refrigerate, 8 hours or overnight.

- **Step 2**

  Heat 1 tablespoon olive oil in a large skillet over medium heat. Cook and stir corn in hot oil until light golden brown and toasted, about 15 minutes.

- **Step 3**

  Mix corn and red pepper together in a bowl. Pour enough dressing over corn mixture to coat completely. Season with salt and black pepper.

- **Step 4**

- Stir basil and a pinch cayenne pepper into corn mixture; toss.

Nutrition:

The nutrition data for this recipe includes the full amount of the dressing ingredients. The actual amount of the dressing consumed will vary.

Nutrition Facts

Per Serving:

314.1 calories; protein 3g 6% DV; carbohydrates 19.4g 6% DV; fat 26.6g 41% DV; cholesterol 7mg 2% DV; sodium 333.1mg 13% DV.

Corn in a Cup (Elote en Vaso)

Prep: 15 mins **Cook:** 5 mins **Total:** 20 mins **Servings:** 10 **Yield:** 10 servings

Ingredients

- 10 ears corn, shucked and kernels removed
- 1 ¼ cups butter
- 2 ½ cups lime juice
- 2 ½ cups crema Mexicana (Mexican cream)
- 1 teaspoon chili powder, or to taste
- 1 pinch salt to taste
- 1 ¼ cups crumbled cotija cheese
- 1 dash hot pepper sauce (such as Valentina), or to taste
- 10 wedges fresh lime

Directions

- **Step 1**

  Place corn in a saucepan and cover with salted water; bring to a boil. Reduce heat to medium-low and simmer until tender, 2 to 3 minutes. Drain and return corn to saucepan.

- **Step 2**

  Spoon 3/4 cup corn into 10 serving bowls; add 2 tablespoons butter to each and stir until butter is melted. Mix 1/4 cup lime juice and 1/4 cup crema Mexicana into each bowl; sprinkle a generous amount of chili powder over each. Season with salt.

- **Step 3**

Top each serving with 2 tablespoons cotija cheese and hot sauce; garnish with a lime wedge.

Nutrition Facts

Per Serving:

563.7 calories; protein 9g 18% DV; carbohydrates 25.8g 8% DV; fat 51.5g 79% DV; cholesterol 159.8mg 53% DV; sodium 406.1mg 16% DV.

Southwestern Roasted Corn Salad

Prep: 20 mins **Cook:** 20 mins **Additional:** 15 mins **Total:** 55 mins **Servings:** 8 **Yield:** 8 servings

Ingredients

- 8 ears fresh corn in husks
- 1 red bell pepper, diced
- 1 green bell pepper, diced
- 1 red onion, chopped
- 1 cup chopped fresh cilantro
- ½ cup olive oil
- 4 cloves garlic, peeled and minced
- 3 lime (2" dia)s limes, juiced
- 1 teaspoon white sugar
- 1 teaspoon salt and pepper to taste
- 1 tablespoon hot sauce

Directions

- **Step 1**

  Place the corn in a large pot with enough water to cover, and soak at least 15 minutes.

- **Step 2**

  Preheat grill for high heat. Remove silks from corn, but leave the husks.

- **Step 3**

  Place corn on the preheated grill. Cook, turning occasionally, 20 minutes, or until tender. Remove from heat, cool slightly, and discard husks.

- **Step 4**

  Cut the corn kernels from the cob, and place in a medium bowl. Mix in the red bell pepper, green bell pepper, and red onion.

- **Step 5**

  In a blender or food processor, mix the cilantro, olive oil, garlic, lime juice, sugar, salt, pepper, and hot sauce. Blend until smooth, and stir into the corn salad.

Nutrition Facts

Per Serving:

223.1 calories; protein 3.7g 8% DV; carbohydrates 23.9g 8% DV; fat 14.7g 23% DV; cholesterolmg; sodium 355.6mg 14% DV.

Pasta with Fresh Tomatoes and Corn

Prep: 20 mins **Cook:** 10 mins **Total:** 30 mins **Servings:** 3 **Yield:** 3 to 4 servings

Ingredients

- 8 ounces pasta
- 4 tablespoons olive oil
- 2 tablespoons red wine vinegar
- ½ cup whole corn kernels, cooked
- 4 medium whole (2-3/5" dia) (blank)s tomatoes, chopped
- ½ cup chopped green onions
- 1 teaspoon dried basil
- salt to taste
- ground black pepper to taste
- 1 tablespoon grated Parmesan cheese
- 2 teaspoons chopped fresh basil

Directions

- **Step 1**

  In a large pot with boiling salted water cook pasta until al dente. Drain.

- **Step 2**

  Meanwhile, in a large bowl whisk together the olive oil, red wine vinegar, and dried basil. Add salt and pepper to taste. Stir in the tomatoes, corn kernels, and scallions. Let sit for 5 to 10 minutes.

- **Step 3**

  Toss pasta with tomato mixture. Sprinkle with grated parmesan cheese. Garnish with fresh basil, if desired.

Nutrition Facts

Per Serving:

439.9 calories; protein 11.8g 24% DV; carbohydrates 53.8g 17% DV; fat 20.9g 32% DV; cholesterol 56mg 19% DV; sodium 61.2mg 2% DV.

Kate's Grilled Corn Salad

Prep: 30 mins **Cook:** 16 mins **Additional:** 5 mins **Total:** 51 mins **Servings:** 8 **Yield:** 8 servings

Ingredients

- 6 ears corn
- 1 tomato, finely chopped
- 5 ounces Monterey Jack cheese, cut into small cubes
- 1 orange bell pepper, finely chopped
- ½ cucumber, finely chopped
- 2 tablespoons finely chopped cilantro
- 1 tablespoon balsamic vinegar
- 1 ½ teaspoons coarse sea salt
- 1 pinch freshly cracked black pepper to taste
- 1 pinch garlic powder, or to taste

Directions

- **Step 1**

  Preheat grill for medium heat and lightly oil the grate.

- **Step 2**

  Bring a large pot of water to a boil. Add corn; cook until tender, about 6 minutes. Drain.

- **Step 3**

  Cook corn on the preheated grill until lightly golden, about 5 minutes. Cool until easily handled, 5 to 10 minutes.

- **Step 4**

  Cut corn kernels off the cob with a sharp knife. Transfer to a large bowl; add tomato, Monterey Jack cheese, orange bell pepper, cucumber, and cilantro. Stir in balsamic vinegar, sea salt, pepper, and garlic powder; mix to combine.

Nutrition Facts

Per Serving:

136.2 calories; protein 7g 14% DV; carbohydrates 15.7g 5% DV; fat 6.3g 10% DV; cholesterol 15.8mg 5% DV; sodium 437.6mg 18% DV.

Roasted Corn and Heirloom Tomato Salad

Prep: 20 mins **Cook:** 15 mins **Additional:** 10 mins **Total:** 45 mins **Servings:** 8 **Yield:** 8 servings

Ingredients

- 4 ears corn on the cob, husks and silk removed
- 2 teaspoons olive oil
- 1 pinch salt and ground black pepper to taste
- 1 red bell pepper
- 1 yellow bell pepper

- 1 ½ pints small heirloom tomatoes, halved
- 1 small red onion, halved and thinly sliced
- 1 bunch fresh basil, coarsely chopped
- 6 ounces mixed salad greens
- 2 tablespoons olive oil, or to taste
- ½ cup balsamic vinegar, or to taste

Directions

- **Step 1**

  Preheat grill for medium heat and lightly oil the grate.

- **Step 2**

  Rub ears of corn with 2 teaspoons olive oil and sprinkle with salt and black pepper; roast the ears on the preheated grill, turning occasionally, until the kernels are lightly browned, 10 to 15 minutes. Place red and yellow bell pepper on the grill and roast until the skins are blistered and lightly charred, turning often, about 15 minutes. Remove corn and bell peppers and let cool.

- **Step 3**

  Cut the kernels from the cobs and place into a large bowl. Peel skins from bell peppers, seed, and cut the peppers into 1-inch pieces; mix peppers and corn together. Lightly toss with heirloom tomatoes, red onion, and basil. Cover and refrigerate until serving time.

- **Step 4**

  Just before serving, mix in the salad greens and drizzle salad with 2 tablespoons olive oil and balsamic vinegar. Lightly toss to coat with dressing and season with salt and black pepper.

Nutrition Facts

Per Serving:

116.5 calories; protein 3g 6% DV; carbohydrates 16.6g 5% DV; fat 5.4g 8% DV; cholesterolmg; sodium 21mg 1% DV.

Refreshing Cucumber Salad

Ingredients

1 h 10 m 4 servings 99 cals

- 2 small cucumbers, thinly sliced
- 1/2 small red onion, thinly sliced
- 1 large tomato, halved and sliced
- 3 tablespoons mayonnaise
- 1 tablespoon white vinegar
- 1/4 teaspoon salt
- 1/2 teaspoon ground black pepper

Directions

Prep 10 m Ready In 1 h 10 m

In a medium bowl, toss together the cucumbers, red onion and tomato. Gently stir in the mayonnaise, vinegar, salt and pepper until coated. Cover and refrigerate for at least 1 hour before serving.

Nutrition Facts

Per Serving: 99 calories; 8.4 g fat; 6 g carbohydrates; 1.1 g protein; 4 mg cholesterol; 208 mg sodium.

Bacon Avocado Salad

Ingredients

20 m 6 servings 427 cals

- 1 pound bacon, chopped
- 1 cucumber, diced
- 1 cup quartered cherry tomatoes
- 1/4 cup seasoned rice vinegar
- salt and ground black pepper to taste
- 5 avocados - peeled, pitted, and diced
- 1/2 cup chopped fresh cilantro
- 4 green onions, chopped

Directions

Prep 20 m Ready In 20 m

- Place bacon in a large skillet and cook over medium-high heat, turning occasionally, until evenly browned, about 10 minutes. Drain bacon on paper towels.
- Stir cucumber, tomatoes, rice vinegar, salt, and pepper together in a bowl. Gently stir bacon, avocado, cilantro, and green onions into cucumber mixture.

Nutrition Facts

Per Serving: 427 calories; 35.1 g fat; 20.5 g carbohydrates; 13.3 g protein; 27 mg cholesterol; 828 mg sodium.

Red Broccoli Salad

Ingredients

1 h 50 m 11 servings 382 cals

- 2 pounds maple-flavored bacon
- 1 large head fresh broccoli, chopped
- 3/4 cup chopped celery
- 1/4 cup minced green onions
- 1/4 cup diced red onion
- 1 1/2 cups seedless grapes, halved

- 3/4 cup blanched slivered almonds
- 1/4 cup white sugar
- 2 tablespoons distilled white vinegar
- 1 cup mayonnaise

Directions

Prep 15 m Cook 35 m Ready In 1 h 50 m

- Place bacon in a large skillet. Cook, turning frequently, over medium high heat until evenly browned. Cool, and then crumble.
- Preheat oven to 300 degrees F (150 degrees C). Spread slivered almonds on a cookie sheet. Bake for approximately 12 to 14 minutes or until lightly browned, turning once during toasting. Cool.
- In a small bowl, mix together mayonnaise, sugar, and vinegar. Set aside.
- In a large bowl, combine broccoli, crumbled bacon, celery, green onions, red onions, grapes, and toasted almonds. Toss with mayonnaise dressing. Chill for several hours in the refrigerator.

Nutrition Facts

Per Serving: 382 calories; 31.2 g fat; 13.7 g carbohydrates; 12.9 g protein; 38 mg cholesterol; 760 mg sodium.

Bacon Ranch Pea Salad

Ingredients

50 m 4 servings 359 cals

- 4 slices bacon
- 1 quart water
- 1 (16 ounce) package frozen green peas
- 1/3 cup chopped onions
- 1/2 cup Ranch dressing
- 1/2 cup shredded Cheddar cheese

Directions

Prep 10 m Cook 10 m Ready In 50 m

- Place bacon in a skillet over medium-high heat, and cook until evenly brown. Drain, crumble, and set aside.
- Bring the water to a boil in a pot. Boil the peas 1 minute, until just tender, and drain. Cool peas under cold running water.
- In a bowl, toss together bacon, peas, onion, Ranch dressing, and Cheddar cheese. Refrigerate 30 minutes or until chilled before serving.

Nutrition Facts

Per Serving: 359 calories; 25.6 g fat; 18.3 g carbohydrates; 14.1 g protein; 36 mg cholesterol; 741 mg sodium.

Almond Mandarin Salad

Ingredients

35 m 8 servings 247 cals

- 1/2 pound bacon
- 2 tablespoons white wine vinegar
- 3 tablespoons honey
- 1/2 teaspoon dry hot mustard
- 1/2 teaspoon celery salt
- 1/2 teaspoon ground paprika
- 1/4 cup olive oil
- 1 head red leaf lettuce, torn into bite-size pieces
- 1 (15 ounce) can mandarin oranges, drained
- 1 bunch green onion, diced
- 3/4 cup slivered almonds

Directions

Prep 20 m Cook 10 m Ready In 35 m

- In a medium skillet over medium-high heat, cook bacon until evenly brown. Drain, cool, and crumble.
- To make the dressing, thoroughly blend the vinegar, honey, dry mustard, celery salt, paprika, and olive oil.
- Place lettuce, oranges, green onion, bacon, and almonds in a serving bowl. Toss with dressing and serve.

Nutrition Facts

Per Serving: 247 calories; 17.6 g fat; 17.5 g carbohydrates; 7.7 g protein; 10 mg cholesterol; 327 mg sodium.

Mediterranean Greek Salad

Ingredients

10 m 8 servings 131 cals

- 3 cucumbers, seeded and sliced
- 1 1/2 cups crumbled feta cheese
- 1 cup black olives, pitted and sliced
- 3 cups diced roma tomatoes
- 1/3 cup diced oil packed sun-dried tomatoes, drained, oil reserved

- 1/2 red onion, sliced

Directions

Prep 10 m Ready In 10 m

- In a large salad bowl, toss together the cucumbers, feta cheese, olives, roma tomatoes, sun-dried tomatoes, 2 tablespoons reserved sun-dried tomato oil, and red onion. Chill until serving.

Nutrition Facts

Per Serving: 131 calories; 8.8 g fat; 9.3 g carbohydrates; 5.5 g protein; 25 mg cholesterol; 486 mg sodium.

Gurkensalat (German Cucumber Salad)

Ingredients

8 h 50 m 8 servings 60 cals

- 2 large cucumbers, sliced thin
- 1/2 onion, sliced thin (optional)
- 1 teaspoon salt
- 1/2 cup sour cream
- 2 tablespoons white sugar
- 2 tablespoons white vinegar
- 1 teaspoon dried dill
- 1 teaspoon dried parsley
- 1 teaspoon paprika

Directions

Prep 20 m Ready In 8 h 50 m

- Spread cucumbers and onion on a platter; season with salt and let rest for 30 minutes. Squeeze excess moisture from cucumbers.
- Stir sour cream, sugar, vinegar, dill, and parsley together in a large bowl.
- Fold cucumber and onion slices into the sour cream mixture.
- Refrigerate 8 hours to over night; garnish with paprika to serve.

Footnotes

- Partner Tip
- Reynolds Aluminum foil can be used to keep food moist, cook it evenly, and make clean-up easier.

Nutrition Facts

Per Serving: 60 calories; 3.1 g fat; 7.9 g carbohydrates; 1.1 g protein; 6 mg cholesterol; 301 mg sodium.

Black Bean and Corn Salad I

Ingredients

12 h 15 m 6 servings 304 cals

- 1/2 cup balsamic vinaigrette salad dressing
- 1/4 teaspoon seasoned pepper
- 1/4 teaspoon dried cilantro
- 1/8 teaspoon ground cayenne pepper
- 1/4 teaspoon ground cumin
- 2 (15 ounce) cans black beans, rinsed and drained
- 2 (15 ounce) cans whole kernel corn, drained
- 1/2 cup chopped onion
- 1/2 cup chopped green onions
- 1/2 cup red bell pepper, chopped

Directions

Prep 15 m Ready In 12 h 15 m

- In a small bowl, mix together vinaigrette, seasoned pepper, cilantro, cayenne pepper, and cumin. Set dressing aside.
- In a large bowl, stir together beans, corn, onion, green onions, and red bell pepper. Toss with dressing. Cover, and refrigerate overnight. Toss again before serving.

Footnotes

- Partner Tip
- Reynolds Aluminum foil can be used to keep food moist, cook it evenly, and make clean-up easier.

Nutrition Facts

Per Serving: 304 calories; 8.5 g fat; 49.5 g carbohydrates; 11.7 g protein; 0 mg cholesterol; 1084 mg sodium.

Barb's Broccoli-Cauliflower Salad

Ingredients

25 m 8 servings 419 cals

- 12 slices bacon
- 1 head fresh broccoli, diced
- 1 head cauliflower, chopped
- 1/2 red onion, diced
- 3/4 cup sunflower seeds
- 1 cup creamy salad dressing
- 1 1/2 tablespoons white wine vinegar
- 1/4 cup white sugar

Directions

Prep 10 m Cook 15 m Ready In 25 m

- Place bacon in a large, deep skillet. Cook over medium high heat until evenly brown. Drain, crumble and set aside.
- Combine the bacon, cauliflower, broccoli, onion and sunflower seeds or pecans.
- Whisk together the salad dressing, vinegar and sugar. Pour over salad and toss to coat. Refrigerate and allow to chill before serving.

Nutrition Facts

Per Serving: 419 calories; 34.1 g fat; 20.2 g carbohydrates; 10.2 g protein; 39 mg cholesterol; 636 mg sodium.

Cucumber Slices With Dill

Ingredients

2 h 15 m 8 servings 120 cals

- 4 large cucumbers, sliced
- 1 onion, thinly sliced
- 1 tablespoon dried dill weed
- 1 cup white sugar
- 1/2 cup white vinegar
- 1/2 cup water
- 1 teaspoon salt (optional)

Directions

Prep 15 m Ready In 2 h 15 m

- In a large serving bowl, combine cucumbers, onions and dill. In a medium size bowl combine sugar, vinegar, water and salt; stir until the sugar dissolves. Pour the liquid mixture over the cucumber mixture. Cover and refrigerate at least 2 hours before serving (the longer this dish marinates the tastier it is!).

Nutrition Facts

Per Serving: 120 calories; 0.3 g fat; 30 g carbohydrates; 1 g protein; 0 mg cholesterol; 295 mg sodium.

Garlic Broccoli

Ingredients

3 h 15 m 8 servings 120 cals

- 4 cloves garlic, peeled
- 1 1/2 teaspoons salt
- 1 bunch broccoli, cut into florets
- 1/3 cup olive oil

- 1/4 cup red wine vinegar
- 1 tablespoon Dijon mustard
- 1/2 cup grated Parmesan cheese, or to taste

Directions

Prep 15 m Cook 3 h Ready In 3 h 15 m

- Place garlic in a mortar dish or on a cutting board, and sprinkle with salt. Mash with a pestle, or use the flat side of a knife to mash garlic and salt into a paste. Transfer to a medium bowl, and stir in olive oil, vinegar, and mustard. Add the broccoli, and stir to coat. Chill for 3 hours to marinate, stirring occasionally. Sprinkle with Parmesan cheese before serving.

Nutrition Facts

Per Serving: 120 calories; 10.6 g fat; 4.1 g carbohydrates; 3.1 g protein; 4 mg cholesterol; 572 mg sodium.

Broccoli Salad I

Ingredients

30 m 8 servings 542 cals

- 1 pound bacon
- 4 cups broccoli florets
- 5 green onions, chopped
- 1/4 cup sunflower seeds
- 1/4 cup golden raisins
- 1 cup mayonnaise
- 1/2 cup white sugar
- 6 tablespoons red wine vinegar

Directions

Prep 15 m Cook 15 m Ready In 30 m

- Place bacon in a large skillet. Cook over medium-high heat until evenly browned. Cool, crumble, and set aside.
- In a large bowl, toss together broccoli, green onions, sunflower seeds, raisins, and bacon.
- In a small bowl, mix together mayonnaise, sugar, and red wine vinegar. Toss with vegetables to coat. Cover, and chill until serving.

Nutrition Facts

Per Serving: 542 calories; 47.6 g fat; 22.1 g carbohydrates; 8.4 g protein; 49 mg cholesterol; 646 mg sodium.

Green Bean and Potato Salad

Ingredients

45 m 10 servings 176 cals

- 1 1/2 pounds red potatoes
- 3/4 pound fresh green beans, trimmed and snapped
- 1/4 cup chopped fresh basil
- 1 small red onion, chopped
- salt and pepper to taste
- 1/4 cup balsamic vinegar
- 2 tablespoons Dijon mustard
- 2 tablespoons fresh lemon juice
- 1 clove garlic, minced
- 1 dash Worcestershire sauce
- 1/2 cup extra virgin olive oil

Directions

Prep 15 m Cook 30 m Ready In 45 m

- Place the potatoes in a large pot, and fill with about 1 inch of water. Bring to a boil, and cook for about 15 minutes, or until potatoes are tender. Throw in the green beans to steam after the first 10 minutes. Drain, cool, and cut potatoes into quarters. Transfer to a large bowl, and toss with fresh basil, red onion, salt and pepper. Set aside. Watch Now
- In a medium bowl, whisk together the balsamic vinegar, mustard, lemon juice, garlic, Worcestershire sauce and olive oil. Pour over the salad, and stir to coat. Taste and season with additional salt and pepper if needed. Watch Now

Nutrition Facts

Per Serving: 176 calories; 11.3 g fat; 17.3 g carbohydrates; 1.9 g protein; 0 mg cholesterol; 97 mg sodium.

Mexican Cucumber Salad

Ingredients

50 m 6 servings 75 cals

- 1 medium cucumber, chopped
- 1 (8.75 ounce) can whole kernel corn, drained
- 1 (16 ounce) can stewed tomatoes, drained and sliced
- 1 green bell pepper, chopped
- 1 red bell pepper, chopped
- 2 tablespoons red wine vinegar
- 1 tablespoon crushed red pepper flakes
- 1/2 teaspoon garlic, minced
- 1/2 teaspoon cumin

- 1/4 teaspoon dried cilantro
- 1/4 teaspoon salt
- 1/8 teaspoon ground black pepper

Directions

Prep 10 m Cook 10 m Ready In 50 m

- In a large bowl, toss together the cucumber, corn, tomatoes, green bell pepper, red bell pepper, and red wine vinegar. Season with crushed red pepper flakes, garlic, cumin, cilantro, salt, and black pepper. Cover, and chill at least 30 minutes before serving.

Nutrition Facts

Per Serving: 75 calories; 1 g fat; 17 g carbohydrates; 2.6 g protein; 0 mg cholesterol; 387 mg sodium.

Zesty Coleslaw

Ingredients

10 m 8 servings 233 cals

- 1/2 cup mayonnaise
- 3/4 cup creamy salad dressing (e.g. Miracle Whip)
- 2 tablespoons prepared horseradish
- 1 1/2 teaspoons white vinegar
- 1 1/2 teaspoons dill weed
- 3 1/2 tablespoons sugar
- 1 (16 ounce) package coleslaw mix

Directions

Prep 10 m Ready In 10 m

- In a large bowl, mix together the mayonnaise, creamy salad dressing, horseradish, vinegar, dill weed and sugar. Add coleslaw mix, and stir to coat. Refrigerate at least 3 hours before serving to blend flavors.

Footnotes

- Partner Tip
- Try using a Reynolds slow cooker liner in your slow cooker for easier cleanup.

Nutrition Facts

Per Serving: 233 calories; 18.4 g fat; 16.4 g carbohydrates; 0.9 g protein; 17 mg cholesterol; 291 mg sodium.

Mediterranean Lentil Salad

Ingredients

30 m 8 servings 147 cals

- 1 cup dry brown lentils
- 1 cup diced carrots
- 1 cup red onion, diced
- 2 cloves garlic, minced
- 1 bay leaf
- 1/2 teaspoon dried thyme
- 2 tablespoons lemon juice
- 1/2 cup diced celery
- 1/4 cup chopped parsley
- 1 teaspoon salt
- 1/4 teaspoon ground black pepper
- 1/4 cup olive oil

Directions

Prep 10 m Cook 20 m Ready In 30 m

- In a saucepan combine lentils, carrots, onion, garlic, bay leaf, and thyme. Add enough water to cover by 1 inch. Bring to boil, reduce heat and simmer uncovered for 15 to 20 minutes or until lentils are tender but not mushy.
- Drain lentils and vegetables and remove bay leaf. Add olive oil, lemon juice, celery, parsley, salt and pepper. Toss to mix and serve at room temperature.

Nutrition Facts

Per Serving: 147 calories; 7.1 g fat; 16.2 g carbohydrates; 6 g protein; 0 mg cholesterol; 453 mg sodium.

Pesto Pasta Caprese Salad

Ingredients

20 m 6 servings 169 cals

- 1 1/2 cups rotini pasta
- 3 tablespoons pesto, or to taste
- 1 tablespoon extra-virgin olive oil
- 1/4 teaspoon salt, or to taste
- 1/4 teaspoon granulated garlic
- 1/8 teaspoon ground black pepper
- 1/2 cup halved grape tomatoes
- 1/2 cup small (pearlini) fresh mozzarella balls
- 2 leaves fresh basil leaves, finely shredded

Directions

Prep 10 m Cook 10 m Ready In 20 m

- Bring a large pot of lightly salted water to a boil; cook the rotini at a boil until tender yet firm to the bite, about 8 minutes; drain.
- Mix pesto, olive oil, salt, granulated garlic, and black pepper in a bowl; add rotini. Toss to coat. Fold in tomatoes, mozzarella, and fresh basil.

Nutrition Facts

Per Serving: 169 calories; 8.3 g fat; 17.1 g carbohydrates; 6.1 g protein; 10 mg cholesterol; 173 mg sodium.

Israeli Salad

Ingredients

25 m 5 servings 271 cals

- 6 cucumbers, diced
- 4 roma (plum) tomatoes, seeded and diced
- 5 green onions, sliced
- 1 red bell pepper, seeded and diced
- 1/3 cup chopped garlic
- 1 cup chopped fresh parsley
- 1/2 cup minced fresh mint leaves
- 1/2 cup olive oil
- 2 tablespoons fresh lemon juice
- 1 tablespoon salt
- 1 tablespoon ground black pepper

Directions

Prep 25 m Ready In 25 m

- Toss the cucumbers, tomatoes, onions, bell pepper, garlic, parsley, and mint together in a bowl. Drizzle the olive oil and lemon juice over the salad and toss to coat. Season with salt and pepper to serve.

Nutrition Facts

Per Serving: 271 calories; 22.3 g fat; 18.4 g carbohydrates; 3.7 g protein; 0 mg cholesterol; 1415 mg sodium.

Easy Seven Layer Vegetable Salad

Ingredients

8 h 10 m 12 servings 471 cals

- 1 head lettuce, torn into small pieces
- 1 (10 ounce) package frozen green peas, thawed
- 1/2 cup chopped green bell pepper

- 12 slices bacon
- 1 1/2 cups small cauliflower florets
- 1/2 cup chopped celery
- 2 cups mayonnaise
- 3 tablespoons white sugar
- 4 ounces shredded Cheddar cheese

Directions

Prep 10 m Ready In 8 h 10 m

- Place bacon in a large, deep skillet. Cook over medium high heat until evenly brown. Drain and set aside. In a 9x13 inch pan layer the lettuce followed by the peas, green pepper, bacon, cauliflower and celery.
- In a small bowl combine the mayonnaise and the sugar. Spread mixture over salad. Sprinkle cheese over top. Cover and chill for at least 8 to 12 hours before serving.

Nutrition Facts

Per Serving: 471 calories; 45 g fat; 10.3 g carbohydrates; 7.9 g protein; 43 mg cholesterol; 539 mg sodium.

Garlicky Beet Delight

Ingredients

30 m 4 servings 141 cals

- 6 medium beets
- 3 tablespoons olive oil
- 2 tablespoons red wine vinegar
- 2 cloves garlic, crushed
- salt to taste

Directions

Prep 10 m Cook 20 m Ready In 30 m

- Wash the beets and boil until tender, about 45 minutes (or 20 minutes in a pressure cooker). Remove the skins by running cold water over the boiled beets, and then slipping of their skins. Slice the beets and toss with the olive oil, vinegar, garlic, and salt.

Footnotes

- Partner Tip
- Reynolds parchment can be used for easier cleanup/removal from the pan.

Nutrition Facts

Per Serving: 141 calories; 10.3 g fat; 11.5 g carbohydrates; 2 g protein; 0 mg cholesterol; 86 mg sodium.

Black-Eyed Pea Salad

Ingredients

8 h 30 m 8 servings 132 cals

- 2 (15.5 ounce) cans black-eyed peas
- 1 large tomato, chopped
- 1 medium red bell pepper, chopped
- 1 medium green bell pepper, chopped
- 1/2 red onion, diced
- 1 stalk celery, chopped
- 1 tablespoon chopped fresh parsley
- 3 tablespoons balsamic vinegar
- 2 tablespoons olive oil
- salt and pepper to taste

Directions

Prep 30 m Ready In 8 h 30 m

- In a medium bowl, toss together black-eyed peas, tomato, red bell pepper, green bell pepper, red onion, celery, and parsley.
- In a small bowl, mix balsamic vinegar and olive oil. Season with salt and pepper. Toss into the vegetables. Cover, and chill in the refrigerator 8 hours, or overnight.

Footnotes

- Partner Tip
- Try using a Reynolds slow cooker liner in your slow cooker for easier cleanup.

Nutrition Facts

Per Serving: 132 calories; 4.1 g fat; 19 g carbohydrates; 5.8 g protein; 0 mg cholesterol; 478 mg sodium.

Byrdhouse Marinated Tomatoes and Mushrooms

Ingredients

3 h 25 m 8 servings 106 cals

- 1/4 cup balsamic vinegar

- 1/3 cup vegetable oil
- 1 1/2 teaspoons white sugar
- 1/2 teaspoon salt
- 1/2 teaspoon ground black pepper
- 12 ounces cherry tomatoes, halved
- 1 (8 ounce) package fresh mushrooms
- 2 green onions, sliced
- 1/2 cup chopped fresh basil

Directions

Prep 25 m Ready In 3 h 25 m

- Whisk together the balsamic vinegar, vegetable oil, sugar, salt, and pepper in a bowl; add the tomatoes, mushrooms, onions, and basil; toss until evenly coated. Cover and chill in refrigerator at least 3 hours. Stir before serving.

Footnotes

- Partner Tip
- Reynolds Aluminum foil can be used to keep food moist, cook it evenly, and make clean-up easier.

Nutrition Facts

Per Serving: 106 calories; 9.4 g fat; 5.3 g carbohydrates; 1.4 g protein; 0 mg cholesterol; 153 mg sodium.

Spicy Italian Salad

Ingredients

4 h 30 m 6 servings 248 cals

- 1/2 cup canola oil
- 1/3 cup tarragon vinegar
- 1 tablespoon white sugar
- 1 teaspoon chopped fresh thyme
- 1/2 teaspoon dry mustard
- 2 cloves garlic, minced
- 1 (8 ounce) can artichoke hearts, drained and quartered
- 5 cups romaine lettuce - rinsed, dried, and chopped
- 1 red bell pepper, cut into strips
- 1 carrot, grated
- 1 red onion, thinly sliced
- 1/4 cup black olives
- 1/4 cup pitted green olives
- 1/2 cucumber, sliced

- 2 tablespoons grated Romano cheese
- ground black pepper to taste

Directions

Prep 30 m Ready In 4 h 30 m

- In a medium container with a lid, mix canola oil, tarragon vinegar, sugar, thyme, dry mustard, and garlic. Cover, and shake until well blended. Place artichoke hearts into the mixture, cover, and marinate in the refrigerator 4 hours, or overnight.
- In a large bowl, toss together lettuce, red bell pepper, carrot, red onion, black olives, green olives, cucumber, and Romano cheese. Season with pepper. Pour in the artichoke and marinade mixture, and toss to coat.

Nutrition Facts

Per Serving: 248 calories; 21.1 g fat; 13.2 g carbohydrates; 3.6 g protein; 3 mg cholesterol; 462 mg sodium.

Deep Dish Layered Salad

Ingredients

55 m 10 servings 396 cals

- 2 eggs
- 1 1/2 heads iceberg lettuce - rinsed, dried, and shredded
- 1 cup chopped celery
- 1 cup chopped green bell pepper
- 1 cup chopped green onions
- 2 cups sliced fresh mushrooms
- 2 cups frozen green peas, thawed
- 2 tablespoons bacon bits
- 2 tablespoons grated Parmesan cheese
- 2 cups mayonnaise
- 2 tablespoons brown sugar
- 1/2 teaspoon garlic powder
- 1/2 teaspoon curry powder

Directions

Prep 20 m Cook 15 m Ready In 55 m

- Place eggs in a saucepan and cover with cold water. Bring water to a boil; cover, remove from heat, and let eggs stand in hot water for 10 to 12 minutes. Remove the eggs from hot water, cool, peel and chop.
- Layer 1/2 of the lettuce in the bottom of a large bowl. Follow with a layer of celery, bell pepper, green onion, mushrooms, peas and egg. Top with remaining lettuce.

- Prepare the dressing by whisking together the mayonnaise, brown sugar, garlic powder and curry powder. Spread evenly over top of salad. Sprinkle with bacon bits and Parmesan cheese. Refrigerate until ready to serve.

Nutrition Facts

Per Serving: 396 calories; 36.9 g fat; 13.1 g carbohydrates; 5.8 g protein; 56 mg cholesterol; 378 mg sodium.

Cucumber and Tomato Salad

Ingredients

15 m 4 servings 98 cals

- 1 tomato, chopped
- 1 cucumber, seeded and chopped
- 1/4 cup thinly sliced red onion
- 1/4 cup canned kidney beans, drained
- 1/4 cup diced firm tofu
- 2 tablespoons chopped fresh basil
- 1/4 cup balsamic vinaigrette salad dressing
- salt and pepper to taste

Directions

Prep 15 m Ready In 15 m

- In a large bowl, combine the tomato, cucumber, red onion, kidney beans, tofu, and basil. Just before serving, toss with balsamic vinaigrette salad dressing, and season with salt and pepper.

Nutrition Facts

Per Serving: 98 calories; 6.1 g fat; 8.6 g carbohydrates; 4.1 g protein; 0 mg cholesterol; 215 mg sodium.

Spring Salad

Ingredients

25 m 8 servings 540 cals

- 12 slices bacon
- 2 heads fresh broccoli, florets only
- 1 cup chopped celery

- 1/2 cup chopped green onions
- 1 cup seedless green grapes
- 1 cup seedless red grapes
- 1/2 cup raisins
- 1/2 cup blanched slivered almonds
- 1 cup mayonnaise
- 1 tablespoon white wine vinegar
- 1/4 cup white sugar

Directions

Prep 10 m Cook 15 m Ready In 25 m

- Place bacon in a large, deep skillet. Cook over medium high heat until evenly brown. Drain, crumble and set aside.
- In a large salad bowl, toss together the bacon, broccoli, celery, green onions, green grapes, red grapes, raisins and almonds.
- Whisk together the mayonnaise, vinegar and sugar. Pour dressing over salad and toss to coat. Refrigerate until ready to serve.

Nutrition Facts

Per Serving: 540 calories; 44.8 g fat; 28.9 g carbohydrates; 9.4 g protein; 39 mg cholesterol; 547 mg sodium.

Tomato Cucumber Salad II

Ingredients

15 m 4 servings 142 cals

- 4 medium fresh tomatoes, cut into 1 inch chunks
- 1 large cucumber, sliced
- 1/2 red onion, diced
- 1/4 cup mayonnaise
- 2 cloves garlic, minced
- 2 teaspoons fresh ground black pepper
- salt to taste

Directions

Prep 15 m Ready In 15 m

- In a large bowl, toss together the tomatoes, cucumber, onion, mayonnaise, and garlic. Season with pepper and salt.

Nutrition Facts

Per Serving: 142 calories; 11.3 g fat; 10.3 g carbohydrates; 2 g protein; 5 mg cholesterol; 87 mg sodium.

Blackberry Spinach Salad

Ingredients

15 m 8 servings 107 cals

- 3 cups baby spinach, rinsed and dried
- 1 pint fresh blackberries
- 6 ounces crumbled feta cheese
- 1 pint cherry tomatoes, halved
- 1 green onion, sliced
- 1/4 cup finely chopped walnuts (optional)
- 1/2 cup edible flowers (optional)

Directions

Prep 15 m Ready In 15 m

- In a large bowl, toss together baby spinach, blackberries, feta cheese, cherry tomatoes, green onion, and walnuts. Garnish with edible flowers.

Nutrition Facts

Per Serving: 107 calories; 7.3 g fat; 7.1 g carbohydrates; 4.8 g protein; 19 mg cholesterol; 250 mg sodium.

Asian Cucumber Salad

Ingredients

1 h 20 m 6 servings 110 cals

- 2 cucumbers - halved lengthwise, seeded, and sliced
- 2 teaspoons salt
- 1/2 cup rice vinegar
- 1/4 cup white sugar
- 2 tablespoons sesame oil
- 1 tablespoon minced garlic
- 1 tablespoon minced fresh ginger root
- 1 tablespoon sesame seeds
- 4 fresh red chile peppers, sliced

Directions

Prep 20 m Ready In 1 h 20 m

- Put the cucumber slices in a colander and sprinkle with salt; set aside to drain for 1 hour.
- Whisk the vinegar and sugar together until the sugar is dissolved; add the sesame oil, garlic, ginger, and sesame seeds; stir.

- Rinse salt off the cucumber slices by running under cold water; place in a large bowl with the sliced red chile peppers. Drizzle the dressing over the vegetables and toss to coat. Serve immediately.

Nutrition Facts

Per Serving: 110 calories; 5.5 g fat; 15.4 g carbohydrates; 1.5 g protein; 0 mg cholesterol; 780 mg sodium.

Cucumbers in Sour Cream

Ingredients

4 h 10 m 12 servings 69 cals

- 2 cucumbers, thinly sliced
- 1 (8 ounce) container sour cream
- 1/4 cup distilled white vinegar
- 1/3 cup white sugar
- salt and ground black pepper to taste

Directions

Prep 10 m Ready In 4 h 10 m

- Place the cucumber slices in a container and cover with cold water. Refrigerate 4 hours to overnight.
- Whisk the sour cream, vinegar, sugar, and salt in a mixing bowl until the sugar has dissolved. Drain the cucumbers and squeeze out the excess water; add to the bowl and mix to coat with dressing.

Footnotes

- Partner Tip
- Reynolds Aluminum foil can be used to keep food moist, cook it evenly, and make clean-up easier.

Nutrition Facts

Per Serving: 69 calories; 4 g fat; 8.1 g carbohydrates; 0.9 g protein; 8 mg cholesterol; 11 mg sodium.

Apple Avocado Salad with Tangerine Dressing

Ingredients

20 m 10 servings 144 cals

- 1 (10 ounce) package baby greens
- 1/4 cup chopped red onion
- 1/2 cup chopped walnuts
- 1/3 cup crumbled blue cheese
- 2 teaspoons lemon zest
- 1 apple - peeled, cored and sliced
- 1 avocado - peeled, pitted and diced
- 4 mandarin oranges, juiced

- 1/2 lemon, juiced
- 1/2 teaspoon lemon zest
- 1 clove garlic, minced
- 2 tablespoons olive oil
- salt to taste

Directions

Prep 20 m Ready In 20 m

- In a large bowl, toss together the baby greens, red onion, walnuts, blue cheese, and lemon zest. Mix in the apple and avocado just before serving.
- In a container with a lid, mix the mandarin orange juice, lemon juice, lemon zest, garlic, olive oil, and salt. Drizzle over the salad as desired.

Nutrition Facts

Per Serving: 144 calories; 11 g fat; 11 g carbohydrates; 3.1 g protein; 3 mg cholesterol; 74 mg sodium.

Spinach Caprese Salad

Ingredients

10 m 2 servings 415 cals

- 1 cup baby spinach leaves
- 1 large tomato, sliced 3/4 inch thick
- 1 ball of fresh mozzarella cheese, sliced
- 2 tablespoons chopped fresh basil
- 1 tablespoon extra-virgin olive oil
- 2 tablespoons balsamic vinegar

Directions

Prep 10 m Ready In 10 m

- Spread the spinach out on a serving plate. Place the slices of tomato on the bed of spinach. Top each slice of tomato with a slice of fresh mozzarella. Sprinkle the basil over the salad and drizzle with olive oil and balsamic vinegar.

Nutrition Facts

Per Serving: 415 calories; 31.4 g fat; 9 g carbohydrates; 21.6 g protein; 89 mg cholesterol; 182 mg sodium.

Super Easy Spinach and Red Pepper Salad

Ingredients

15 m 6 servings 128 cals

- 1 (6 ounce) package baby spinach
- 1 red bell pepper, chopped
- 1/2 cup grated Parmesan cheese
- 1/4 cup olive oil
- 1/4 cup rice vinegar

Directions

Prep 15 m Ready In 15 m

- In a large bowl, mix the baby spinach, red bell pepper, and Parmesan cheese.
- In a small bowl, mix the olive oil and rice vinegar. Toss with the baby spinach mixture, and serve.

Nutrition Facts

Per Serving: 128 calories; 11.6 g fat; 2.6 g carbohydrates; 4.2 g protein; 7 mg cholesterol; 151 mg sodium.

Green Bean Blue Cheese Salad

Ingredients

1 h 30 m 4 servings 419 cals

- 1 pound fresh green beans, cut into 2 inch pieces
- 1/4 cup blue cheese, crumbled
- 1/4 red onion, thinly sliced
- 1/2 cup olive oil
- 4 tablespoons balsamic vinegar
- 1/2 cup pecan pieces, toasted
- salt and pepper to taste

Directions

Prep 20 m Cook 10 m Ready In 1 h 30 m

- Place green beans in a steamer over 1 inch of boiling water, and cover. Cook until tender but still firm, about 2 to 6 minutes. Allow to cool.
- In a medium bowl, combine beans, onion, blue cheese, and pecans. Stir in olive oil and balsamic vinegar. Season with salt and pepper. Chill for at least an hour before serving.

Nutrition Facts

Per Serving: 419 calories; 40.3 g fat; 13.3 g carbohydrates; 5.4 g protein; 6 mg cholesterol; 275 mg sodium.

Twenty-Four Hour Salad

Ingredients

1 d 20 m 6 servings 640 cals

- 6 cups shredded iceberg lettuce
- 1/2 cup chopped celery
- 1/2 cup chopped green bell pepper
- 1/2 cup chopped onions
- 1/2 cup frozen green peas, thawed and drained
- 1 1/2 cups mayonnaise
- 2 tablespoons white sugar
- 2 cups shredded Cheddar cheese
- 1 (3 ounce) can bacon bits

Directions

Prep 20 m Ready In 1 d 20 m

- In a large transparent bowl, layer lettuce, celery, bell peppers, onions, peas, mayonnaise, sugar and cheese. Sprinkle bacon bits evenly over the top of the salad.
- Cover bowl, and refrigerate for 24 hours before serving.

Nutrition Facts

Per Serving: 640 calories; 59.3 g fat; 11.9 g carbohydrates; 17.3 g protein; 70 mg cholesterol; 1015 mg sodium.

Apple Coleslaw

Ingredients

8 h 15 m 6 servings 99 cals

- 4 cups shredded cabbage
- 1 cup shredded carrot
- 1 Granny Smith apple - peeled, cored and coarsely shredded
- 2 tablespoons honey
- 1 tablespoon brown sugar
- 2 teaspoons white vinegar
- 1 tablespoon pineapple juice (optional)
- 2 tablespoons mayonnaise
- 1 dash salt
- 1 teaspoon ground black pepper

Directions

Prep 15 m Ready In 8 h 15 m

- Place the shredded cabbage and carrot together in a bowl with the sliced apple, and toss to combine. In a separate bowl, stir together the honey, brown sugar, vinegar, pineapple juice, and mayonnaise until the honey and sugar have dissolved completely. Pour over the salad, and toss to coat. Season with salt and pepper, and toss again. Cover and chill until ready to serve.

Footnotes

- Note
- Do not substitute sweetened sandwich spread for regular mayonnaise or the cole slaw will become too sweet.

Nutrition Facts

Per Serving: 99 calories; 3.8 g fat; 17.1 g carbohydrates; 1.1 g protein; 2 mg cholesterol; 118 mg sodium.

Creamy Cauliflower Salad

Ingredients

30 m 6 servings 408 cals

- 1 head cauliflower, cut into florets
- 1/2 cup grape tomatoes, quartered
- 3 tablespoons bacon bits
- 1/4 cup shredded Cheddar cheese
- 3 hard-boiled eggs, chopped
- 1 cup mayonnaise
- 1/3 cup sugar
- 2 tablespoons vinegar
- 1 tablespoon lemon juice

Directions

Prep 15 m Cook 15 m Ready In 30 m

- Place egg in a saucepan and cover with cold water. Bring water to a boil and immediately remove from heat. Cover and let eggs stand in hot water for 10 to 12 minutes. Remove from hot water, cool, peel, and chop.
- Toss cauliflower florets, tomatoes, bacon bits, cheese, and eggs together in a bowl.
- In a separate bowl, dissolve sugar into vinegar and lemon. Whisk in mayonnaise until thoroughly combined.
- Pour dressing over salad, and toss gently to coat. Cover and refrigerate until well-chilled. Toss again gently, and serve.

Nutrition Facts

Per Serving: 408 calories; 34.6 g fat; 18.5 g carbohydrates; 8.4 g protein; 128 mg cholesterol; 415 mg sodium.

Cilantro, Avocado, Tomato, and Feta Salad

Ingredients

25 m 10 servings 195 cals

- 8 roma (plum) tomatoes, diced
- 3 jalapeno peppers, seeded and diced
- 3 bunches green onion, sliced
- 4 ounces crumbled garlic and herb feta cheese
- 4 avocados - peeled, pitted and diced
- 2 tablespoons fresh lemon juice
- 3 bunches cilantro, chopped
- salt and ground black pepper to taste

Directions

Prep 25 m Ready In 25 m

- Combine the tomatoes, jalapeno peppers, green onion, and feta cheese in a large bowl; toss together. Add the diced avocado; drizzle the lemon juice over the avocado to keep it from turning brown. Stir in the cilantro. Season with salt and pepper. Mix well and serve.

Nutrition Facts

Per Serving: 195 calories; 14.5 g fat; 15.5 g carbohydrates; 6 g protein; 8 mg cholesterol; 169 mg sodium.

Cucumber, Tomato, and Red Onion Salad

Ingredients

20 m 6 servings 41 cals

- 4 tomatoes, cut into 8 wedges
- 2 large cucumbers, peeled and sliced
- 1 large red onion, chopped
- 1/4 cup chopped fresh cilantro
- juice of 1 fresh lime
- salt to taste

Directions

Prep 20 m Ready In 20 m

- Mix the tomatoes, cucumbers, red onion, cilantro, and lime juice together in a bowl. Season with salt to serve.

Nutrition Facts

Per Serving: 41 calories; 0.3 g fat; 9.5 g carbohydrates; 1.7 g protein; 0 mg cholesterol; 8 mg sodium.

Cilantro Cucumber Salad

Ingredients

40 m 3 servings 26 cals

- 2 cucumbers
- 2 tablespoons fresh lime juice
- 1 teaspoon chili powder
- 1/4 teaspoon salt
- 1 tablespoon chopped fresh cilantro

Directions

Prep 10 m Ready In 40 m

- Peel cucumbers, slice lengthwise into quarters, and cut into 1 inch pieces; place in large bowl. Sprinkle with lime juice, chili powder, and salt; toss. Toss with cilantro. Refrigerate until chilled.

Nutrition Facts

Per Serving: 26 calories; 0.3 g fat; 6.2 g carbohydrates; 1 g protein; 0 mg cholesterol; 206 mg sodium.

Tortellini Pesto Salad

Ingredients

1 h 30 m 6 servings 383 cals

- 1 (9 ounce) package cheese tortellini
- 1 small red bell pepper, julienned
- 3/4 cup broccoli florets, blanched
- 1/3 cup shredded carrots
- 1/3 cup pitted green olives
- 1 clove garlic, chopped
- 1/2 cup mayonnaise
- 1/4 cup prepared basil pesto
- 1/4 cup milk
- 2 tablespoons grated Parmesan cheese
- 1 tablespoon olive oil
- 1 tablespoon distilled white vinegar
- 1 bunch fresh spinach leaves

Directions

Prep 15 m Cook 8 m Ready In 1 h 30 m

- Bring a large pot of lightly salted water to a boil. Place tortellini in the pot, and cook for 7 to 8 minutes, until al dente. Drain, and cool.
- In a large bowl, mix the cooked tortellini, red bell pepper, broccoli, carrots, olives, and garlic.
- In a separate bowl, stir together the mayonnaise, pesto, milk, Parmesan cheese, olive oil, and vinegar. Pour over the tortellini and vegetables, and gently toss to coat. Cover, and place in the refrigerator 1 hour, until chilled. Serve over spinach leaves.

Nutrition Facts

Per Serving: 383 calories; 27.3 g fat; 26.1 g carbohydrates; 11.2 g protein; 31 mg cholesterol; 615 mg sodium.

Red Quinoa and Avocado Salad

Ingredients

50 m 2 servings 311 cals

- 1/3 cup red quinoa
- 2/3 cup water
- 1 cup cherry tomatoes, halved
- 1/2 cup diced cucumber
- 1/4 cup diced red onion
- 2 tablespoons lime juice
- 1/2 teaspoon ground cumin seed
- salt and pepper to taste
- 2 cups baby spinach leaves
- 1 avocado - peeled, pitted and sliced

Directions

Prep 5 m Cook 15 m Ready In 50 m

- Bring the quinoa and water to a boil in a saucepan over high heat. Reduce heat to medium-low, cover, and simmer until the quinoa is tender, and the water has been absorbed, about 15 to 20 minutes. Spread into a mixing bowl, and refrigerate until cold.
- Once the quinoa has chilled, gently stir in the tomatoes, cucumber, and onion. Season with lime juice, cumin, salt, and pepper; stir to combine. Divide the spinach leaves onto salad plates, and top with the quinoa salad. Garnish with the avocado slices to serve.

Footnotes

Cook's Note

Be sure to rinse the quinoa thoroughly before cooking as there is a bitter coating on the grains. Regular quinoa can be used in place of the red quinoa (they taste the same). Red quinoa is usually found in the Organic section of most grocers or also in bulk food type stores.

Nutrition Facts

Per Serving: 311 calories; 17.3 g fat; 37.1 g carbohydrates; 8.1 g protein; 0 mg cholesterol; 46 mg sodium.

Broccoli Salad

Ingredients

8 servings 49 cals

- 4 cups fresh broccoli florets
- 1/4 cup red onion, finely diced
- 3 tablespoons raisins
- 2 tablespoons dry roasted sunflower seeds
- 1/4 cup plain yogurt
- 2 tablespoons orange juice
- 1 tablespoon fat-free mayonnaise

Directions

- Combine the broccoli, onions, raisins, and sunflower seeds.
- In a small bowl, whisk the yogurt, orange juice, and mayonnaise until blended. Pour over the broccoli mixture and toss to coat.

Nutrition Facts

Per Serving: 49 calories; 1.5 g fat; 8.2 g carbohydrates; 2.2 g protein; < 1 mg cholesterol; 41 mg sodium.

Cool Cucumber and Avocado Salad

Ingredients

20 m 6 servings 146 cals

- 2 English (hothouse) cucumbers, diced
- 1 teaspoon salt
- 1/2 cup diced red onion
- 1 small red bell pepper, diced
- 2 limes, zested and juiced
- 1/4 cup chopped fresh cilantro
- 1 tablespoon white sugar
- 1/2 teaspoon curry powder
- 4 dashes hot pepper sauce
- 2 avocados - peeled, pitted and diced

Directions

Prep 20 m Ready In 20 m

- Place the cucumber slices into a colander set in the sink, and sprinkle with salt. Set aside and allow to drip.
- In a salad bowl, mix together the red onion, red bell pepper, lime zest and juice, cilantro, sugar, curry powder, and hot pepper sauce until thoroughly combined and the sugar has dissolved. Drain the cucumber slices, and pat them dry with paper towels. Stir the cucumbers into the salad. Gently toss the avocados with the salad and serve.

Footnotes

- Cook's Notes
- If you are not going to serve this immediately do not peel, chop and add the avocado until just before serving. Also, if you are in a real hurry, you can skip draining the cucumbers, but any leftovers you have will get watery.

Nutrition Facts

Per Serving: 146 calories; 10.1 g fat; 15.8 g carbohydrates; 2.4 g protein; 0 mg cholesterol; 414 mg sodium.

Cucumber Salad With Thai Sweet Chili Vinaigrette

Ingredients

1 h 15 m 4 servings 36 cals

- 2 tablespoons rice vinegar
- 2 tablespoons Thai sweet chili sauce
- 1 teaspoon sesame oil
- 1/4 teaspoon white sugar
- 1/4 teaspoon granulated garlic
- 1 pinch salt to taste
- 1 cucumber, thinly sliced
- 1 green onion, thinly sliced

Directions

Prep 15 m Ready In 1 h 15 m

- Whisk rice vinegar, chili sauce, sesame oil, sugar, and garlic together in a small bowl; season with salt.
- Combine cucumber and onion in a separate bowl. Pour vinegar mixture over cucumber and onion mixture and toss to coat. Refrigerate at least 1 hour. Toss before serving.

Nutrition Facts

Per Serving: 36 calories; 1.3 g fat; 6.5 g carbohydrates; 0.6 g protein; 0 mg cholesterol; 87 mg sodium.

Tomato Mozzarella Salad

Ingredients

10 m 6 servings 199 cals

- 3 large tomatoes, sliced
- 8 ounces mozzarella cheese, sliced
- 1/4 cup olive oil
- 1/4 cup balsamic vinegar
- 1/4 teaspoon salt
- 1/8 teaspoon ground black pepper
- 1/4 cup minced fresh basil

Directions

Prep 10 m Ready In 10 m

- Place tomato slices, alternating with mozzarella slices, on a large serving platter.
- Combine oil, balsamic vinegar, salt, and pepper in a jar with a tight-fitting lid; shake well. Drizzle over tomatoes and mozzarella; sprinkle with basil.

Footnotes

- Partner Tip
- Reynolds Aluminum foil can be used to keep food moist, cook it evenly, and make clean-up easier.

Nutrition Facts

Per Serving: 199 calories; 15.2 g fat; 6.2 g carbohydrates; 10.1 g protein; 24 mg cholesterol; 338 mg sodium.

Easy Cucumber Salad

Ingredients

4 h 20 m 4 servings 25 cals

- 2 tablespoons white vinegar
- 1 tablespoon chopped fresh parsley
- 1 tablespoon chopped fresh dill
- 1 teaspoon minced garlic
- 1 tablespoon white sugar
- 1 teaspoon salt
- 1 seedless cucumber, peeled and chopped

Directions

Prep 20 m Ready In 4 h 20 m

- Whisk together the vinegar, parsley, dill, garlic, sugar, and salt in a bowl; add the cucumber and stir to coat. Cover and chill in refrigerator 4 to 8 hours. Stir well before serving.

Nutrition Facts

Per Serving: 25 calories; 0.1 g fat; 6 g carbohydrates; 0.6 g protein; 0 mg cholesterol; 584 mg sodium.

Cottage Cheese Salad

Ingredients

10 m 4 servings 138 cals

- 1 (16 ounce) container cottage cheese, drained
- 4 roma (plum) tomatoes, chopped
- 4 green onions, chopped
- 2 medium cucumbers, peeled and diced
- salt and pepper to taste

Directions

Prep 10 m Ready In 10 m

- In a medium bowl, stir together the cottage cheese, tomatoes, green onions, and cucumbers. Season with salt and pepper to taste. Chill until serving.

Nutrition Facts

Per Serving: 138 calories; 5.2 g fat; 8.3 g carbohydrates; 15 g protein; 17 mg cholesterol; 459 mg sodium.

Broccoli Raisin Salad

Ingredients

1 h 25 m 12 servings 330 cals

- 1 pound bacon
- 6 cups chopped broccoli
- 1 small red onion, finely chopped
- 1 cup raisins
- 1 cup mayonnaise
- 1/2 cup white sugar
- 2 tablespoons white vinegar
- 1 (3 ounce) package sunflower seeds

Directions

Prep 15 m Cook 10 m Ready In 1 h 25 m

- Place bacon in a large skillet and cook over medium-high heat, turning occasionally, until evenly browned, about 10 minutes. Drain the bacon slices on paper towels and cool. Chop bacon.
- Mix broccoli, bacon, red onion, and raisins in a bowl.
- Whisk mayonnaise, sugar, and vinegar together in a bowl; stir dressing into broccoli mixture until evenly coated. Cover bowl and refrigerate for flavors to blend, about 1 hour. Sprinkle salad with sunflower seeds.

Nutrition Facts

Per Serving: 330 calories; 23.6 g fat; 24.8 g carbohydrates; 7.9 g protein; 21 mg cholesterol; 408 mg sodium.

Cucumber Salad I

Ingredients

10 m 4 servings 47 cals

- 2 cucumbers, peeled and thinly sliced
- 1/2 red onion, thinly sliced
- 1 1/2 cups water
- 1/2 cup rice wine vinegar
- 1 teaspoon white sugar
- 1/4 teaspoon seasoning salt

Directions

Prep 10 m Ready In 10 m

- Combine cucumbers and red onion in a salad bowl.
- In a small bowl, stir together water, rice wine vinegar, sugar, and seasoned salt. Pour over vegetables. Chill for 1 hour. Serve chilled or at room temperature.

Nutrition Facts

Per Serving: 47 calories; 0.2 g fat; 11.3 g carbohydrates; 0.7 g protein; 0 mg cholesterol; 691 mg sodium.

Asian Cucumber Thai Salad

Ingredients

1 h 20 m 4 servings 169 cals

- 1/3 cup distilled white vinegar
- 1/3 cup white sugar
- 1/2 teaspoon ground coriander
- 1/2 teaspoon crushed red pepper flakes
- 1/2 teaspoon salt

- 2 pounds cucumbers - halved, seeded, and sliced
- 1/2 cup finely chopped red onion
- 2 roma (plum) tomatoes, chopped
- 2 tablespoons chopped fresh cilantro
- 2 tablespoons chopped fresh mint
- 1/4 cup chopped roasted peanuts
- fresh mint sprigs (optional)

Directions

Prep 20 m Ready In 1 h 20 m

- Whisk together the vinegar, sugar, coriander, red pepper flakes, and salt in a salad bowl until the sugar is dissolved. Stir in the cucumbers, onion, tomatoes, cilantro, and chopped mint, and toss to coat with dressing. Cover and refrigerate for 1 hour to blend the flavors.
- Before serving, toss again with chopped peanuts, and garnish with sprigs of fresh mint.

Footnotes

- Partner Tip
- Reynolds Aluminum foil can be used to keep food moist, cook it evenly, and make clean-up easier.

Nutrition Facts

Per Serving: 169 calories; 5 g fat; 30.5 g carbohydrates; 4.3 g protein; 0 mg cholesterol; 299 mg sodium.

Amazing Cucumber Basil Salad

Prep: 15 mins **Additional:** 8 hrs **Total:** 8 hrs 15 mins **Servings:** 12 **Yield:** 12 servings

Ingredients

- 2 cups fresh baby spinach
- 2 tablespoons chopped fresh basil
- 1 pound campari tomatoes, seeded and minced
- 2 large seedless cucumbers, peeled and minced
- 1 large red onion, minced
- 3 cloves garlic, minced
- 1 teaspoon salt, or to taste
- 1 teaspoon cracked black pepper, or to taste

Directions

- **Step 1**

  Run spinach and basil through a food processor until finely chopped.
- **Step 2**

  Mix spinach mixture, tomatoes, cucumbers, red onion, garlic, salt, and pepper together in a large bowl with an air-tight lid. Cover bowl and refrigerate salad, 8 hours to overnight.

Cook's Note:

The liquid from this salad can be strained off, mixed with a bit of balsamic vinegar and olive oil, and used a a delicious dressing for a green salad.

Nutrition Facts

Per Serving:

20.2 calories; protein 1g 2% DV; carbohydrates 4.4g 1% DV; fat 0.2g; cholesterolmg; sodium 201.3mg 8% DV.

Marinated Cherry Tomato Salad

Prep: 10 mins **Additional:** 2 hrs **Total:** 2 hrs 10 mins **Servings:** 7 **Yield:** 6 to 8 servings

Ingredients

- 4 cups halved cherry tomatoes
- ¼ cup vegetable oil
- 3 tablespoons cider vinegar
- 1 teaspoon dried parsley
- 1 teaspoon dried basil
- 1 teaspoon dried oregano
- ½ teaspoon salt
- 1 ½ teaspoons white sugar

Directions

- **Step 1**

  In a small bowl or cup measure, mix together oil, apple cider vinegar, herbs, salt, and sugar.

- **Step 2**

  Pour dressing over cherry tomatoes in a serving dish, and gently stir to coat. Chill for at least 2 hours. Gently stir from bottom to top, coating all tomatoes, before serving.

Nutrition Facts

Per Serving:

93.5 calories; protein 0.8g 2% DV; carbohydrates 5.2g 2% DV; fat 8.2g 13% DV; cholesterolmg; sodium 174.5mg 7% DV.

Summer Corn Salad

Prep: 25 mins **Cook:** 20 mins **Total:** 45 mins **Servings:** 4 **Yield:** 4 servings

Ingredients

- 6 ears corn, husked and cleaned
- 3 large tomatoes, diced
- 1 large onion, diced
- ¼ cup chopped fresh basil

- ¼ cup olive oil
- 2 tablespoons white vinegar
- salt and pepper to taste

Directions

- **Step 1**

  Bring a large pot of lightly salted water to a boil. Cook corn in boiling water for 7 to 10 minutes, or until desired tenderness. Drain, cool, and cut kernels off the cob with a sharp knife.

- **Step 2**

  In a large bowl, toss together the corn, tomatoes, onion, basil, oil, vinegar, salt and pepper. Chill until serving.

Nutrition Facts

Per Serving:

305.5 calories; protein 6.2g 12% DV; carbohydrates 42.8g 14% DV; fat 15.6g 24% DV; cholesterolmg; sodium 8.7mg.

Grilled Corn Salad

Prep: 15 mins **Cook:** 10 mins **Additional:** 45 mins **Total:** 1 hr 10 mins **Servings:** 6 **Yield:** 6 servings

Ingredients

- 6 ears freshly shucked corn
- 1 green pepper, diced
- 2 medium (blank)s Roma (plum) tomatoes, diced
- ¼ cup diced red onion
- ½ bunch fresh cilantro, chopped, or more to taste
- 2 teaspoons olive oil, or to taste
- 1 pinch salt and ground black pepper to taste

Directions

- **Step 1**

  Preheat an outdoor grill for medium heat; lightly oil the grate.

- **Step 2**

  Cook the corn on the preheated grill, turning occasionally, until the corn is tender and specks of black appear, about 10 minutes; set aside until just cool enough to handle. Slice the kernels off of the cob and place into a bowl.

- **Step 3**

  Combine the warm corn kernels with the green pepper, diced tomato, onion, cilantro, and olive oil. Season with salt and pepper; toss until evenly mixed. Set aside for at least 30 minutes to allow flavors to blend before serving.

Nutrition Facts

Avocado Salad

Prep: 10 mins **Total:** 10 mins **Servings:** 6 **Yield:** 6 servings

Ingredients

- 2 avocado, NS as to Florida or Californias avocados - peeled, pitted and diced
- 1 sweet onion, chopped
- 1 green bell pepper, chopped
- 1 large ripe tomato, chopped
- ¼ cup chopped fresh cilantro
- ½ lime, juiced
- salt and pepper to taste

Directions

- **Step 1**

  In a medium bowl, combine avocados, onion, bell pepper, tomato, cilantro and lime juice. Gently toss until evenly coated. Season with salt and pepper.

Nutrition Facts

Per Serving:

126.1 calories; protein 2.1g 4% DV; carbohydrates 10.2g 3% DV; fat 10g 15% DV; cholesterolmg; sodium 8.5mg.

Portable Chinese Chicken Salad

Prep: 5 mins **Cook:** 20 mins **Total:** 25 mins **Servings:** 11 **Yield:** 10 to 12 servings

Ingredients

- 4 breast half, bone and skin removed (blank)s skinless, boneless chicken breast halves
- 1 (16 ounce) package coleslaw mix
- 2 (3 ounce) packages chicken flavored ramen noodles, crushed, seasoning packet reserved
- ½ cup blanched slivered almonds
- ½ cup corn oil
- ½ cup rice garlic vinegar
- 1 packet artificial sweetener

Directions

- **Step 1**

Saute chicken in a large skillet until well browned. Place coleslaw in a large bowl, add chicken and set aside (or refrigerate if not serving soon).

- **Step 2**

Break up ramen noodles into a small bowl; add almonds and set aside.

- **Step 3**

In a small bowl combine the corn oil, vinegar, ramen seasoning packets and artificial sweetener. Mix well and set aside until ready to serve.

- **Step 4**

When you arrive at your destination, add noodle mixture and dressing mixture to large chicken/coleslaw bowl and stir together. Serve with a smile!

Nutrition Facts

Per Serving:

265.7 calories; protein 13.6g 27% DV; carbohydrates 18.6g 6% DV; fat 15.1g 23% DV; cholesterol 29.4mg 10% DV; sodium 427.3mg 17% DV.

Chicken Mango Salsa Salad with Chipotle Lime Vinaigrette

Prep: 30 mins **Total:** 30 mins **Servings:** 6 **Yield:** 6 servings

Ingredients

- 1 mango - peeled, seeded and diced
- 2 medium (blank)s roma (plum) tomatoes, chopped
- ½ onion, chopped
- 1 jalapeno pepper, seeded and chopped - or to taste
- ¼ cup cilantro leaves, chopped
- 1 lime, juiced
- ½ cup olive oil
- ¼ cup lime juice
- ¼ cup white sugar
- ½ teaspoon ground chipotle chile powder
- ½ teaspoon ground cumin
- ¼ teaspoon garlic powder
- 1 (10 ounce) bag baby spinach leaves
- 1 cup broccoli coleslaw mix
- 1 cup diced cooked chicken
- 3 tablespoons diced red bell pepper
- 3 tablespoons diced green bell pepper

- 2 tablespoons diced yellow bell pepper
- 2 tablespoons dried cranberries
- 2 tablespoons chopped pecans
- 2 tablespoons crumbled blue cheese

Directions

- **Step 1**

  Mix mango, tomatoes, onion, jalapeno pepper, cilantro, and juice of 1 lime in a large bowl; set aside.

- **Step 2**

  Whisk olive oil, 1/4 cup lime juice, sugar, chipotle chile powder, cumin, and garlic powder together in a bowl; set aside.

- **Step 3**

  Toss spinach leaves, broccoli coleslaw mix, chicken, red, green, and yellow bell peppers, cranberries, and pecans together in a large bowl.

- **Step 4**

  Spread mango salsa and blue cheese on top.

- **Step 5**

  Drizzle lime dressing over salad and toss before serving.

Cook's Note:

I recommend prechopping bell peppers and salsa ingredients in advance to save time. I also recommend using a broccoli slaw mix that includes shredded carrots and red cabbage because it makes for a beautifully colorful salad.

Nutrition Facts

Per Serving:

316.8 calories; protein 7.6g 15% DV; carbohydrates 25g 8% DV; fat 22.3g 34% DV; cholesterol 13.8mg 5% DV; sodium 109.9mg 4% DV.

Thai Chicken Broccoli Slaw

Prep: 10 mins **Cook:** 20 mins **Total:** 30 mins **Servings:** 4 **Yield:** 4 servings

Ingredients

- 2 tablespoons olive oil
- 2 large skinless, boneless chicken breast halves, cut into bite-size pieces
- 1 (12 ounce) package broccoli coleslaw mix
- 1 teaspoon sesame oil, or to taste
- ½ cup water
- ½ cup peanut sauce (such as House of Tsang), or to taste
- 1 pinch salt to taste

Directions

- **Step 1**

  Heat olive oil in a skillet over medium-high heat; cook and stir chicken until no longer pink in the center and juices run clear, about 5 minutes. Add broccoli slaw mix, sesame oil, and water; simmer on medium-low heat until liquid is reduced and broccoli slaw is tender, about 15 minutes. Fold in peanut sauce and salt.

Nutrition Facts

Per Serving:

315.1 calories; protein 28.3g 57% DV; carbohydrates 8.2g 3% DV; fat 18.9g 29% DV; cholesterol 64.6mg 22% DV; sodium 178.4mg 7% DV.

Beefy Cabbage Stew

Cook: 1 hr 15 mins **Total:** 1 hr 15 mins **Servings:** 8 **Yield:** 8 servings

Ingredients

- 1 pound extra-lean ground beef
- 1 (15 ounce) can pinto beans
- 1 (15 ounce) can kidney beans
- 1 (10 ounce) can diced tomatoes with green chile peppers
- 1 (14.5 ounce) can Italian-style diced tomatoes
- 1 (15 ounce) can whole kernel corn, drained
- 1 (11.5 ounce) can tomato juice
- 1 ½ cups water
- 1 (16 ounce) package coleslaw mix
- 1 teaspoon Greek-style seasoning

Directions

- **Step 1**

  In a large pot over medium heat, cook beef until brown; drain.

- **Step 2**

  Return meat to pot with pinto beans, kidney beans, diced tomatoes with green chiles, Italian-style diced tomatoes, tomato juice, water, coleslaw mix and Greek seasoning. Simmer over low heat 1 hour.

Nutrition Facts

Per Serving:

283.2 calories; protein 18.1g 36% DV; carbohydrates 35.4g 11% DV; fat 8.4g 13% DV; cholesterol 38.8mg 13% DV; sodium 813mg 33% DV.

Catfish Po Boy

Prep: 30 mins **Cook:** 10 mins **Total:** 40 mins **Servings:** 8 **Yield:** 4 sandwiches

Ingredients

Coleslaw:

- 1 (16 ounce) package shredded coleslaw mix
- ¼ cup pickled pepperoncini peppers, chopped
- ¼ cup diced red onion
- ⅓ cup mayonnaise
- ½ lemon, juiced
- 1 tablespoon red wine vinegar
- 1 teaspoon Dijon mustard
- 1 teaspoon white sugar
- 1 teaspoon salt
- 1 tablespoon granulated garlic
- ½ teaspoon granulated onion
- ¼ teaspoon lemon pepper

Catfish:

- 8 (3 ounce) fillets catfish
- 2 tablespoons hot sauce (such as Tabasco)
- ½ cup Cajun seasoning
- 2 cups all-purpose flour
- 2 cups cornmeal
- 2 cups bread crumbs
- 1 tablespoon granulated garlic
- 1 tablespoon granulated onion
- 1 ½ teaspoons ground black pepper
- ½ teaspoon cayenne pepper
- 1 cup olive oil for frying

Assembly:

- 4 eaches Italian-style hoagie buns, split lengthwise
- 1 cup remoulade-style sandwich spread (see footnote for recipe link)
- 1 lemon, cut into wedges
- 1 cup cherry tomato halves
- ½ cup banana pepper rings

Directions

- **Step 1**

Combine coleslaw mix, pepperoncini peppers, red onion, mayonnaise, lemon juice, red wine vinegar, Dijon mustard, sugar, salt, 1/2 teaspoon granulated garlic, 1/2 teaspoon granulated onion, and lemon pepper in a large bowl. Toss until well combined. Cover and refrigerate until ready to use.

- **Step 2**
  Place catfish fillets in a large shallow baking dish. Sprinkle hot sauce over the top and turn the fillets to coat.

- **Step 3**
  Combine Cajun seasoning, flour, cornmeal, bread crumbs, 1 tablespoon granulated garlic, 1 tablespoon granulated onion, black pepper, and cayenne pepper in a large brown paper bag. Add catfish fillets and shake gently to coat fillets thoroughly.

- **Step 4**
  Heat olive oil in a large skillet over medium-high heat. Fry breaded catfish fillets until browned and crisp, about 3 minutes per side. Place on paper towel-lined paper plates to drain.

- **Step 5**
  Spread each hoagie bun with 1/4 cup remoulade-style spread. Place 2 catfish fillets on top and top with 1 to 2 cups coleslaw. Garnish with lemon wedge, cherry tomato halves, and banana pepper rings.

Nutrition Facts

Per Serving:

1069.7 calories; protein 29.8g 60% DV; carbohydrates 128.7g 42% DV; fat 48.6g 75% DV; cholesterol 72.2mg 24% DV; sodium 2961.1mg 118% DV.

Timesaver Kale Slaw

Prep: 15 mins **Total:** 15 mins **Servings:** 12 **Yield:** 6 cups

Ingredients

- ⅓ cup balsamic vinegar
- ⅓ cup extra-virgin olive oil
- 2 tablespoons honey
- 1 lime, juiced
- 1 (16 ounce) bag coleslaw mix
- 5 ounces baby kale, chopped into bite-size pieces
- ½ red onion, finely chopped
- 2 tablespoons sunflower seeds, or more to taste
- 1 pinch salt and ground black pepper to taste

Directions

- **Step 1**
  Whisk balsamic vinegar, olive oil, honey, and lime juice in a large bowl. Add coleslaw mix, baby kale, red onion, and sunflower seeds; toss to combine. Season with salt and pepper.

Nutrition Facts

Per Serving:

117.8 calories; protein 1.3g 3% DV; carbohydrates 10.8g 4% DV; fat 8.1g 12% DV; cholesterol 3mg 1% DV; sodium 28.9mg 1% DV.

Golompke (Beef and Cabbage Casserole)

Prep: 15 mins **Cook:** 1 hr 15 mins **Total:** 1 hr 30 mins **Servings:** 8 **Yield:** 8 servings

Ingredients

- 1 pound ground beef
- 1 small onion, chopped
- 1 (16 ounce) bag coleslaw mix
- ¾ cup uncooked white rice
- 2 (10.75 ounce) cans condensed tomato soup
- 1 (10.75 ounce) can water

Directions

- **Step 1**

  Preheat an oven to 375 degrees F (190 degrees C).

- **Step 2**

  Heat a large skillet over medium-high heat, and stir in the ground beef and onion. Cook and stir until the beef is crumbly, evenly browned, and no longer pink. Drain and discard any excess grease.

- **Step 3**

  Layer the coleslaw mix, rice, and ground beef in a 9x13 inch baking dish. Combine the soup and water in a medium bowl. Pour the soup over the top of the ground beef. Cover with foil.

- **Step 4**

  Bake for 1 hour and 15 minutes, or until the rice is tender.

Nutrition Facts

Per Serving:

267.7 calories; protein 13g 26% DV; carbohydrates 32.6g 11% DV; fat 9.4g 15% DV; cholesterol 39mg 13% DV; sodium 470.1mg 19% DV.

Thai Shrimp and Cabbage

Prep 5 m Cook 10 m Ready In 15 m

Ingredients

- 1 cup shredded cabbage

- 3 teaspoons vegetable oil, divided
- 1 slice onion, halved
- 1 garlic clove, minced
- 8 uncooked large shrimp, peeled and deveined
- 2 tablespoons water
- 1 tablespoon soy sauce
- 1 tablespoon minced fresh cilantro
- 1/8 teaspoon crushed red pepper flakes

Directions

- In a small skillet, stir-fry the cabbage in 1 teaspoon oil for 2 minutes or until tender. Remove and keep warm. In the same skillet, stir-fry onion and garlic in remaining oil until tender. Add the shrimp, water and soy sauce; stir-fry for 2-3 minutes or until shrimp turn pink. Stir in cilantro and pepper flakes. Serve over cabbage.

Weeknight Crack Slaw

Prep 15M Cook 10M Ready In 25 m

Ingredients

- 1 tablespoon chipotle hot sauce (such as Cholula)
- 1 tablespoon rice vinegar
- 1 tablespoon soy sauce
- 1 1/2 teaspoons minced ginger
- 1 teaspoon agave syrup
- 1 tablespoon olive oil
- 1 tablespoon sesame oil
- 1 pound ground turkey
- 1/2 teaspoon salt
- 1/2 tablespoon ground black pepper
- 1 (8 ounce) package coleslaw mix
- 1/2 red bell pepper, diced
- 2 green onions, chopped, or more to taste
- 2 cloves garlic, minced
- 1 tablespoon sesame seeds

Directions

- Mix chipotle hot sauce, rice vinegar, soy sauce, ginger, and agave syrup together in a small bowl to make sauce.

- Heat olive oil and sesame oil in a wok or large skillet over medium heat. Add ground turkey; cook, stirring to break up clumps, until juices run clear, about 6 minutes. Season with salt and pepper. Transfer to a bowl, reserving juices in the wok.
- Combine coleslaw mix, red bell pepper, green onions, and garlic in the wok; cook and stir over medium heat until slaw is slightly wilted, 1 to 2 minutes. Add sauce; mix to combine, about 1 minute. Return turkey to the wok and stir until heated through, 2 to 3 minutes.
- Sprinkle sesame seeds over slaw before serving.

Footnotes

Cook's Notes:

Substitute ginger paste for the minced ginger if desired.

Substitute white sugar for the agave syrup if desired.

Use coleslaw mix with red cabbage and carrots for maximum color and vegetable variety.

Nutrition Facts

Per Serving: 302 calories; 18 g fat; 12.5 g carbohydrates; 24.3 g protein; 88 mg cholesterol; 682 mg sodium.

Grilled Corn and Red Cabbage Slaw

Prep: 15 mins **Cook:** 15 mins **Total:** 30 mins **Servings:** 4 **Yield:** 4 servings

Ingredients

- 2 ears fresh sweet corn, husks removed
- 1 lime, juiced
- ½ cup chopped cilantro
- ½ teaspoon ground cumin
- 1 pinch salt
- 1 pinch ground black pepper to taste
- 1 tablespoon olive oil
- ½ head red cabbage, shredded
- 1 jalapeno pepper, seeded and diced
- ¼ cup crumbled queso fresco

Directions

- **Step 1**

  Preheat an outdoor grill for medium-high heat and lightly oil the grate.

- **Step 2**

  Place corn on hot grill and cook until charred on all sides, about 15 minutes. Remove corn from grill and cool.

- **Step 3**

Pour lime juice into a bowl; add cilantro, cumin, salt, and pepper. Pour olive oil into lime juice mixture while continuously whisking until dressing is smooth. Add cabbage and jalapeno pepper to dressing and toss.

- **Step 4**

Cut corn from cob and mix into cabbage mixture. Crumble queso fresco over slaw; toss well.

Cook's Note:

For ease in removing corn from cob, place the narrow end of cob in a fluted tube pan (such as Bundt(R)). This gives you a holder for the cob and it catches the removed corn kernels.

Nutrition Facts

Per Serving:

132.4 calories; protein 5.2g 10% DV; carbohydrates 19.6g 6% DV; fat 5.5g 9% DV; cholesterol 5mg 2% DV; sodium 58.9mg 2% DV.

Grilled Corn Off the Cob Salad

Prep: 10 mins **Cook:** 20 mins **Additional:** 12 hrs **Total:** 12 hrs 30 mins **Servings:** 6 **Yield:** 6 servings

Ingredients

- 12 ears fresh corn with husks
- 5 stalks celery, diced
- ½ green bell pepper, diced
- 1 small onion, diced
- 2 tablespoons chopped pimento peppers
- ½ cup olive oil
- 2 tablespoons balsamic vinegar
- 1 teaspoon sea salt
- 1 teaspoon Dijon mustard
- 1 teaspoon white sugar
- 1 pinch ground black pepper to taste

Directions

- **Step 1**
- Preheat an outdoor grill for medium heat, and lightly oil the grate.
- **Step 2**
- Grill corn on preheated grill until husks are charred on all sides, about 20 minutes. Remove corn from grill and allow to cool.
- **Step 3**

Remove husks and silk from corn, then cut corn kernels from the cob.
- **Step 4**

Toss corn kernels, celery, green bell pepper, onion, and pimento peppers together in a large bowl.

- **Step 5**

  Whisk olive oil, balsamic vinegar, sea salt, Dijon mustard, sugar, and black pepper together in a bowl.

- **Step 6**

  Pour dressing into the corn mixture and toss well. Cover and refrigerate for at least 12 hours and up to 3 days before serving.

Nutrition Facts

Per Serving:

334.1 calories; protein 6.3g 13% DV; carbohydrates 38.7g 13% DV; fat 20.2g 31% DV; cholesterolmg; sodium 370.9mg 15% DV.

Hatch Chile Corn

Prep: 10 mins **Cook:** 20 mins **Additional:** 5 mins **Total:** 35 mins **Servings:** 4 **Yield:** 4 servings

Ingredients

- 4 ears fresh corn, shucked
- 1 Hatch chile pepper
- ⅓ cup crumbled goat cheese
- 1 tablespoon lime juice
- 1 pinch salt and ground black pepper to taste

Directions

- **Step 1**
- Preheat an outdoor grill for medium heat, and lightly oil the grate.
- **Step 2**
- Cook corn and chile pepper on the preheated grill until corn is slightly charred and chile pepper is blistered, about 20 minutes.
- **Step 3**
- Place chile pepper in a resealable plastic bag. Let steam until softened, about 5 minutes. Peel skin off chile pepper and chop.
- **Step 4**
- Cut corn kernels off the cob into a large bowl. Stir in chopped chile pepper, goat cheese, lime juice, salt, and black pepper.

Cook's Note:

Substitute another type of green chile pepper for the Hatch if desired.

Nutrition Facts

Per Serving:

127.3 calories; protein 5.8g 12% DV; carbohydrates 19.2g 6% DV; fat 4.5g 7% DV; cholesterol 9.2mg 3% DV; sodium 113.5mg 5% DV.

Angie's Dad's Best Cabbage Coleslaw

Ingredients

30 m 20 servings 131 cals

- 1 medium head cabbage, shredded
- 1 large red onion, diced
- 1 cup grated carrots
- 2 stalks celery, chopped
- 1 cup white sugar
- 1 cup white vinegar
- 3/4 cup vegetable oil
- 1 tablespoon salt
- 1 tablespoon dry mustard
- black pepper to taste

Directions

Prep 30 m Ready In 30 m

- In a large bowl, combine cabbage, onion, carrots, and celery. Sprinkle with 1 cup sugar, and mix well. In a small saucepan, combine vinegar, oil, salt, dry mustard, and pepper. Bring to a boil. Pour hot dressing over cabbage mixture, and mix well.

Footnotes

Cook's Note:

This is best if made a day ahead to 2 weeks ahead. If you make it far ahead, drain juice prior to serving.

Nutrition Facts

Per Serving: 131 calories; 8.4 g fat; 14.1 g carbohydrates; 0.9 g protein; 0 mg cholesterol; 364 mg sodium.

Marinated Cucumber, Onion, and Tomato Salad

Ingredients

2 h 15 m 6 servings 156 cals

- 1 cup water
- 1/2 cup distilled white vinegar
- 1/4 cup vegetable oil
- 1/4 cup sugar
- 2 teaspoons salt
- 1 tablespoon fresh, coarsely ground black pepper
- 3 cucumbers, peeled and sliced 1/4-inch thick
- 3 tomatoes, cut into wedges

- 1 onion, sliced and separated into rings

Directions

Prep 15 m Ready In 2 h 15 m

- Whisk water, vinegar, oil, sugar, salt, and pepper together in a large bowl until smooth; add cucumbers, tomatoes, and onion and stir to coat.
- Cover bowl with plastic wrap; refrigerate at least 2 hours.

Nutrition Facts

Per Serving: 156 calories; 9.5 g fat; 18 g carbohydrates; 1.8 g protein; 0 mg cholesterol; 784 mg sodium.

Black Bean Salad

Ingredients

20 m 12 servings 159 cals

- 1 (15 ounce) can black beans, rinsed and drained
- 2 (15 ounce) cans whole kernel corn, drained
- 8 green onions, chopped
- 2 jalapeno peppers, seeded and minced
- 1 green bell pepper, chopped
- 1 avocado - peeled, pitted, and diced
- 1 (4 ounce) jar pimentos
- 3 tomatoes, seeded and chopped
- 1 cup chopped fresh cilantro
- 1 lime, juiced
- 1/2 cup Italian salad dressing
- 1/2 teaspoon garlic salt

Directions

Prep 20 m Ready In 20 m

- In a large bowl, combine the black beans, corn, green onions, jalapeno peppers, bell pepper, avocado, pimentos, tomatoes, cilantro, lime juice, and Italian dressing. Season with garlic salt. Toss, and chill until serving.

Nutrition Facts

Per Serving: 159 calories; 6.3 g fat; 24.2 g carbohydrates; 5 g protein; 0 mg cholesterol; 562 mg sodium.

Mom's Cucumber Salad

Ingredients

15 m 8 servings 237 cals

- 1 cup mayonnaise
- 1/4 cup white sugar
- 4 teaspoons distilled white vinegar
- 1/2 teaspoon dried dill weed
- 1/2 teaspoon seasoned salt
- 4 medium cucumbers, peeled and sliced

Directions

Prep 15 m Ready In 15 m

- In a large bowl, stir together the mayonnaise, sugar, vinegar, dill, and seasoned salt. Mix in the cucumber slices, tossing to coat.

Nutrition Facts

Per Serving: 237 calories; 22 g fat; 10.8 g carbohydrates; 0.9 g protein; 10 mg cholesterol; 216 mg sodium.

Strawberry Avocado Salad

Ingredients

15 m 2 servings 610 cals

- 2 tablespoons white sugar
- 2 tablespoons olive oil
- 4 teaspoons honey
- 1 tablespoon cider vinegar
- 1 teaspoon lemon juice
- 2 cups torn salad greens
- 1 avocado - peeled, pitted and sliced
- 10 strawberries, sliced
- 1/2 cup chopped pecans

Directions

Prep 15 m Ready In 15 m

- In a small bowl, whisk together the sugar, olive oil, honey, vinegar, and lemon juice. Set aside.
- Place the salad greens in a pretty bowl, and top with sliced avocado and strawberries. Drizzle dressing over everything, then sprinkle with pecans. Refrigerate for up to 2 hours before serving, or serve immediately.

Nutrition Facts

Per Serving: 610 calories; 50 g fat; 44 g carbohydrates; 6.1 g protein; 0 mg cholesterol; 23 mg sodium.

Roasted Beets with Feta

Ingredients

1 h 15 m 4 servings 149 cals

- 4 beets, trimmed, leaving 1 inch of stems attached
- 1/4 cup minced shallot
- 2 tablespoons minced fresh parsley
- 2 tablespoons extra-virgin olive oil
- 1 tablespoon balsamic vinegar
- 1 tablespoon red wine vinegar
- salt and pepper to taste
- 1/4 cup crumbled feta cheese

Directions

Prep 15 m Cook 45 m Ready In 1 h 15 m

- Preheat oven to 400 degrees F (200 degrees C). Wrap each beet individually in aluminum foil, and place onto a baking sheet.
- Bake beets in preheated oven until easily pierced with a fork, 45 minutes to 1 hour. Once done, remove from oven, and allow to cool until you can handle them. Peel beets, and cut into 1/4 inch slices.
- While the beets are roasting, whisk together shallot, parsley, olive oil, balsamic vinegar, and red wine vinegar in a bowl until blended; season to taste with salt and pepper, and set aside.
- To assemble the dish, place the warm, sliced beets onto a serving dish, pour vinaigrette over the beets, and sprinkle with feta cheese before serving.

Footnotes

- Partner Tip
- Reynolds Aluminum foil can be used to keep food moist, cook it evenly, and make clean-up easier.

Nutrition Facts

Per Serving: 149 calories; 10.3 g fat; 11.1 g carbohydrates; 3.9 g protein; 14 mg cholesterol; 243 mg sodium.

Ali's Greek Tortellini Salad

Ingredients

2 h 30 m 8 servings 486 cals

- 2 (9 ounce) packages cheese tortellini
- 1/2 cup extra virgin olive oil
- 1/4 cup lemon juice
- 1/4 cup red wine vinegar
- 2 tablespoons chopped fresh parsley
- 1 teaspoon dried oregano
- 1/2 teaspoon salt

- 6 eggs
- 1 pound baby spinach leaves
- 1 cup crumbled feta cheese
- 1/2 cup slivered red onion

Directions

Prep 15 m Cook 15 m Ready In 2 h 30 m

- Bring a large pot of lightly salted water to a boil. Add tortellini, and cook for 7 minutes or until al dente; drain.
- In a large bowl, mix the olive oil, lemon juice, red wine vinegar, parsley, oregano, and salt. Place the cooked tortellini in the bowl, and toss to coat. Cover, and chill at least 2 hours in the refrigerator.
- Place eggs in a saucepan with enough water to cover, and bring to a boil. Remove from heat, and allow eggs to sit in the hot water for 10 to 12 minutes. Drain, cool, peel, and quarter.
- Gently mix the spinach, feta cheese, and onion into the bowl with the pasta. Arrange the quartered eggs around the salad to serve.

Nutrition Facts

Per Serving: 486 calories; 30.3 g fat; 35.7 g carbohydrates; 19.8 g protein; 196 mg cholesterol; 836 mg sodium.

Avocado and Tuna Tapas

Ingredients

20 m 4 servings 294 cals

- 1 (12 ounce) can solid white tuna packed in water, drained
- 1 tablespoon mayonnaise
- 3 green onions, thinly sliced, plus additional for garnish
- 1/2 red bell pepper, chopped
- 1 dash balsamic vinegar
- black pepper to taste
- 1 pinch garlic salt, or to taste
- 2 ripe avocados, halved and pitted

Directions

Prep 20 m Ready In 20 m

- Stir together tuna, mayonnaise, green onions, red pepper, and balsamic vinegar in a bowl. Season with pepper and garlic salt, then pack the avocado halves with the tuna mixture. Garnish with reserved green onions and a dash of black pepper before serving.

Nutrition Facts

Per Serving: 294 calories; 18.2 g fat; 11 g carbohydrates; 23.9 g protein; 27 mg cholesterol; 154 mg sodium.

Caribbean Sweet Potato Salad

Ingredients

1 h 5 servings 231 cals

- 1 large russet potato, peeled and quartered
- 1 large sweet potato, peeled and quartered
- 1 cup corn
- 1 teaspoon prepared Dijon-style mustard
- 2 tablespoons fresh lime juice
- 3 tablespoons chopped fresh cilantro
- 1 clove garlic, minced
- 3 tablespoons canola oil
- 1/2 teaspoon salt
- 1/4 teaspoon ground black pepper
- 1 cucumber, halved lengthwise and chopped
- 1/2 red onion, thinly sliced
- 1/4 cup finely chopped peanuts

Directions

Prep 30 m Cook 30 m Ready In 1 h

- Place the Russet potato pieces into a large saucepan, and cover with salted water. Bring to a boil, turn the heat down, and simmer for 10 minutes. Add the sweet potato, and cook about 15 minutes more. Remove a piece of each potato, and cut it in half to see if it is cooked enough. Once the potatoes are tender, add corn kernels; cook another 30 seconds. Drain through a colander. Fill the saucepan with cold water, and drop vegetables into water. Cool for 5 minutes, and drain.
- In a large bowl, whisk together mustard, lime juice, cilantro, and garlic. Slowly whisk in oil. Mix in salt and black pepper.
- Cut cooled potatoes into 1 inch cubes, and add to dressing along with cucumber, and red onion. Toss well. Serve at room temperature or chilled. Toss the peanuts in just before serving.

Nutrition Facts

Per Serving: 231 calories; 12.6 g fat; 27.8 g carbohydrates; 4.6 g protein; 0 mg cholesterol; 290 mg sodium.

Orzo and Tomato Salad with Feta Cheese

Ingredients

25 m 6 servings 329 cals

- 1 cup uncooked orzo pasta
- 1/4 cup pitted green olives

- 1 cup diced feta cheese
- 3 tablespoons chopped fresh parsley
- 3 tablespoons chopped fresh dill
- 1 ripe tomato, chopped
- 1/4 cup virgin olive oil
- 1/8 cup lemon juice
- salt and pepper to taste

Directions

Prep 15 m Cook 10 m Ready In 25 m

- Bring a large pot of lightly salted water to a boil. Cook orzo for 8 to 10 minutes, or until al dente; drain, and rinse with cold water.
- When orzo is cool, transfer to a medium bowl and mix in olives, feta cheese, parsley, dill, and tomato. In a small bowl, whisk together oil and lemon juice. Pour over pasta, and mix well. Season with salt and pepper to taste. Chill before serving.

Nutrition Facts

Per Serving: 329 calories; 19.6 g fat; 28.1 g carbohydrates; 10.9 g protein; 37 mg cholesterol; 614 mg sodium.

Cherry Tomato Salad

Ingredients

1 h 20 m 6 servings 341 cals

- 40 cherry tomatoes, halved
- 1 cup pitted and sliced green olives
- 1 (6 ounce) can black olives, drained and sliced
- 2 green onions, minced
- 3 ounces pine nuts
- 1/2 cup olive oil
- 2 tablespoons red wine vinegar
- 1 tablespoon white sugar
- 1 teaspoon dried oregano
- salt and pepper to taste

Directions

Prep 15 m Cook 5 m Ready In 1 h 20 m

- In a big bowl, combine cherry tomatoes, green olives, back olives, and spring onion.
- In a dry skillet, toast pine nuts over medium heat until golden brown, turning frequently. Stir into tomato mixture.

- In a small bowl, mix together olive oil, red wine vinegar, sugar, and oregano. Season to taste with salt and pepper. Pour over salad, and gently stir to coat. Chill for 1 hour.

Nutrition Facts

Per Serving: 341 calories; 32.2 g fat; 12.6 g carbohydrates; 5.1 g protein; 0 mg cholesterol; 940 mg sodium.

Dave's Coleslaw

Ingredients

8 h 20 m 12 servings 215 cals

- 1 head cabbage, cored and coarsely chopped
- 1 carrot, grated
- 1 sweet onion, minced
- 3 green onions, minced
- 1 dill pickle, minced
- 1 cup mayonnaise
- 2 cups buttermilk
- 2 tablespoons dill pickle juice
- 2 tablespoons vinegar
- 2 tablespoons prepared yellow mustard
- 1/2 cup white sugar
- 1 pinch cayenne pepper
- 1 teaspoon salt, divided
- 1 clove garlic

Directions

Prep 20 m Ready In 8 h 20 m

- In a large bowl, mix the cabbage, carrot, sweet onion, green onions, and dill pickle.
- In a separate bowl, whisk together the mayonnaise, buttermilk, dill pickle juice, vinegar, mustard, sugar, cayenne pepper, and 3/4 teaspoon salt. Mash together the remaining salt and garlic, and whisk into the dressing. Drizzle dressing over the slaw, and toss to coat. Cover and refrigerate 8 hours, or overnight, before serving.

Nutrition Facts

Per Serving: 215 calories; 15.2 g fat; 18.7 g carbohydrates; 3.2 g protein; 9 mg cholesterol; 462 mg sodium.

Tomato Cucumber Salad

Ingredients

10 m 4 servings 31 cals

- 2 tomatoes, chopped
- 1 cucumber, peeled and diced
- 1 onion, chopped
- 1 tablespoon lemon juice
- salt to taste
- ground black pepper to taste

Directions

Prep 10 m Ready In 10 m

- Combine tomatoes, cucumbers, and onions in a salad bowl. Season to taste with salt and black pepper. Sprinkle with lemon juice. Chill.

Footnotes

- Partner Tip
- Try using a Reynolds slow cooker liner in your slow cooker for easier cleanup.

Nutrition Facts

Per Serving: 31 calories; 0.3 g fat; 7.1 g carbohydrates; 1.3 g protein; 0 mg cholesterol; 6 mg sodium.

Cilantro Tomato Corn Salad

Ingredients

20 m 4 servings 174 cals

- 3 ears fresh corn in husks
- 1/4 cup butter, melted
- 2 roma (plum) tomatoes, chopped
- 1 jalapeno pepper, seeded and finely chopped
- 1/2 small red onion, finely chopped
- 2 cloves garlic, minced
- 1/2 bunch fresh cilantro, chopped
- salt and freshly ground black pepper to taste
- 1 pinch salt-free lemon-herb seasoning (such as Mrs. Dash)

Directions

Prep 15 m Cook 5 m Ready In 20 m

- Peel back corn husks, but leave them attached at the bottom. Remove the silks, and fold husks back up over the corn. Place on a dinner plate, and cook in the microwave for 5 minutes on High power, turning corn once half way through. Cool until cool enough to touch, then slice corn kernels from the cob and place them in a serving bowl.
- Stir butter into the corn along with the tomatoes, jalapeno, red onion, garlic and cilantro. Season with salt, pepper, and seasoning blend. Mix well, taste, and adjust seasoning if necessary. Some people like the salad warm, but I prefer to chill it a little before serving.

Nutrition Facts

Per Serving: 174 calories; 12.4 g fat; 15.8 g carbohydrates; 3 g protein; 31 mg cholesterol; 97 mg sodium.

Greek Pasta Salad with Shrimp, Tomatoes, Zucchini, Peppers, and Feta

Ingredients

1 h 22 m 6 servings 802 cals

- Dijon Vinaigrette
- 1/4 cup rice wine vinegar
- 2 tablespoons Dijon mustard
- 1 large clove garlic, minced
- Big pinch of salt
- Black pepper, to taste
- 2/3 cup extra-virgin olive oil
- Pasta Salad
- 2 medium zucchini, thinly sliced lengthwise
- 1 medium yellow pepper, halved lengthwise, seeded
- 2 tablespoons olive oil
- Ground black pepper and salt, to taste
- 1 gallon water
- 2 tablespoons salt
- 1 pound medium pasta shells
- 1 pound cooked shrimp, halved lengthwise
- 8 ounces cherry tomatoes, halved
- 3/4 cup coarsely chopped, pitted Kalamata olives
- 1 cup crumbled feta cheese
- 1/2 small red onion, cut into small dice
- 2 teaspoons dried oregano

Directions

Prep 35 m Cook 17 m Ready In 1 h 22 m

- To make the vinaigrette, whisk together the rice wine vinegar, mustard, garlic, pinch of salt, and pepper; slowly pour in 2/3 cup olive oil, whisking constantly. Pour into a jar with a tight-fitting lid to transport it to the picnic.
- Adjust oven rack to highest position and turn broiler on high. Toss zucchini and bell pepper with 2 tablespoons olive oil and salt and pepper to taste, and arrange on a large baking sheet with sides. Broil

until spotty brown, 8 to 10 minutes, turning zucchini slices and pepper halves once. Set aside in a large bowl to cool, then cut into bite-sized pieces.
- Bring 1 gallon of water and 2 tablespoons of salt to boil. Add pasta; boil using package times, until just tender. Drain thoroughly (do not rinse) and dump onto the baking sheet. Set aside to cool.
- Put vegetables, pasta and remaining ingredients (except dressing) in the bowl or a gallon-sized zipper bag (can be refrigerated for several hours). When ready to serve, add dressing; toss to coat.

Nutrition Facts

Per Serving: 802 calories; 45.7 g fat; 65.8 g carbohydrates; 33.6 g protein; 185 mg cholesterol; 3398 mg sodium.

Insalata Caprese I

Ingredients

1 h 15 m 4 servings 498 cals

- 4 ripe tomatoes, cut into wedges
- 14 ounces fresh mozzarella cheese, diced
- 1 red onion, sliced
- 1/3 cup extra virgin olive oil
- 1/3 cup balsamic vinegar
- 1/4 cup chopped fresh basil
- salt and pepper to taste

Directions

Prep 15 m Ready In 1 h 15 m

- In a large bowl, combine the tomatoes, cheese, onion, oil, vinegar, basil, and salt and pepper to taste. Toss and chill for 1 hour. Serve on large platter.

Nutrition Facts

Per Serving: 498 calories; 40.3 g fat; 12.7 g carbohydrates; 19.3 g protein; 78 mg cholesterol; 154 mg sodium.

Korean Cucumber Salad

Ingredients

25 m 2 servings 98 cals

- 1/4 cup white vinegar
- 1/4 teaspoon black pepper
- 1/2 teaspoon red pepper flakes
- 1 teaspoon vegetable oil
- 2 tablespoons sesame seeds

- 1 cucumber, thinly sliced
- 1/2 green onion, sliced
- 1/2 carrot, julienned

Directions

Prep 20 m Cook 5 m Ready In 25 m

- In a medium bowl, stir together vinegar, black pepper, and red pepper flakes.
- Heat oil in a saucepan over medium-high heat. Stir in sesame seeds, and reduce heat to medium. Cook until seeds are brown, about 5 minutes. Remove seeds with a slotted spoon, and stir into vinegar mixture. Mix in cucumber, green onions, and carrot. Cover, and refrigerate at least 5 minutes.

Nutrition Facts

Per Serving: 98 calories; 7 g fat; 8.1 g carbohydrates; 2.6 g protein; 0 mg cholesterol; 14 mg sodium.

Avocado and Tomato Salad

Ingredients

1 h 15 m 6 servings 356 cals

- 4 large tomatoes, chopped
- 4 avocados - peeled, pitted and diced
- 1 red onion, thinly sliced
- 1/4 teaspoon ground black pepper, or to taste
- 1 (8 ounce) bottle balsamic vinaigrette salad dressing

Directions

Prep 15 m Ready In 1 h 15 m

- In a large serving bowl, toss together the tomatoes, avocados and red onion. Dust lightly with black pepper, and pour salad dressing over. Cover and chill for at least one hour before serving to blend flavors.

Nutrition Facts

Per Serving: 356 calories; 31.9 g fat; 20.2 g carbohydrates; 3.8 g protein; 0 mg cholesterol; 482 mg sodium.

California Salad Bowl

Ingredients

25 m 8 servings 321 cals

- 1 avocado, peeled and pitted
- 1 tablespoon lemon juice
- 1/2 cup mayonnaise
- 1/4 teaspoon hot pepper sauce

- 1/4 cup olive oil
- 1 clove garlic, peeled and minced
- 1/2 teaspoon salt
- 1 head romaine lettuce- rinsed, dried and torn into bite sized pieces
- 3 ounces Cheddar cheese, shredded
- 2 tomatoes, diced
- 2 green onions, chopped
- 1/4 (2.25 ounce) can pitted green olives
- 1 cup coarsely crushed corn chips

Directions

Prep 25 m Ready In 25 m

- In a blender or food processor, mix avocado, lemon juice, mayonnaise, hot pepper sauce, olive oil, garlic, and salt. Process until smooth.
- In a large bowl, toss together romaine lettuce, Cheddar cheese, tomatoes, green onions, green olives, and corn chips. Toss with the avocado dressing mixture just before serving.

Nutrition Facts

Per Serving: 321 calories; 28.7 g fat; 13.5 g carbohydrates; 4.9 g protein; 16 mg cholesterol; 419 mg sodium.

P.J.'s Fresh Corn Salad

Ingredients

1 h 15 m 8 servings 141 cals

- 8 ears fresh corn
- 1 tomato, chopped
- 1 zucchini, chopped
- 1 cucumber, peeled and chopped
- 1 red onion, chopped
- 1 red bell pepper, chopped
- 1/2 cup Italian-style salad dressing

Directions

Prep 15 m Ready In 1 h 15 m

- Husk the corn and slice the kernels from the cob. In a large bowl, mix together the corn, tomato, zucchini, cucumber, onion and red bell pepper. Pour dressing over vegetables and toss to coat. Refrigerate until chilled, at least 1 hour.

Nutrition Facts

Per Serving: 141 calories; 5.4 g fat; 23 g carbohydrates; 3.9 g protein; 0 mg cholesterol; 261 mg sodium.

Broccoli Salad IV

Ingredients

30 m 6 servings 367 cals

- 1/4 cup bacon bits
- 1 head fresh broccoli florets
- 1 cup shredded Cheddar cheese
- 1/2 cup raisins
- 1/2 cup hulled sunflower seeds
- 1 red onion, chopped
- 1 cup creamy salad dressing, e.g. Miracle Whip ™
- 1/4 cup white sugar

Directions

Prep 30 m Ready In 30 m

- Place bacon in a large, deep skillet. Cook over medium high heat until evenly brown. Drain, crumble and set aside.
- In a large bowl, mix together the bacon, broccoli, cheese, raisins, onion and sunflower seeds.
- In a small bowl, whisk together the creamy salad dressing and sugar. Pour over broccoli mixture and toss well to coat. Cover and refrigerate until chilled.

Nutrition Facts

Per Serving: 367 calories; 23.5 g fat; 31.1 g carbohydrates; 10.7 g protein; 36 mg cholesterol; 616 mg sodium.

Carrot and Raisin Salad II

Ingredients

30 m 4 servings 343 cals

- 1/2 cup sour cream
- 1/2 cup light mayonnaise
- 1 tablespoon lemon juice
- 1/2 teaspoon salt
- 1 tablespoon brown sugar
- 4 cups shredded carrot
- 1 cup raisins

Directions

Prep 30 m Ready In 30 m

- In a large bowl, whisk together the sour cream, mayonnaise, lemon juice, salt and brown sugar. Add carrots and raisins and stir until coated.

Nutrition Facts

Per Serving: 343 calories; 16.3 g fat; 50.6 g carbohydrates; 3.4 g protein; 23 mg cholesterol; 624 mg sodium.

Mediterranean Zucchini and Chickpea Salad

Ingredients

25 m 6 servings 258 cals

- 2 cups diced zucchini
- 1 (15 ounce) can chickpeas, drained and rinsed
- 1 cup halved grape tomatoes
- 3/4 cup chopped red bell pepper
- 1/2 cup chopped sweet onion (such as Vidalia®)
- 1/2 cup crumbled feta cheese
- 1/2 cup chopped Kalamata olives
- 1/3 cup olive oil
- 1/3 cup packed fresh basil leaves, roughly chopped
- 1/4 cup white balsamic vinegar
- 1 tablespoon chopped fresh rosemary
- 1 tablespoon capers, drained and chopped
- 1 clove garlic, minced
- 1/2 teaspoon dried Greek oregano
- 1 pinch crushed red pepper flakes (optional)
- salt and ground black pepper to taste

Directions

Prep 25 m Ready In 25 m

- Mix zucchini, chickpeas, tomatoes, red bell pepper, onion, feta, Kalamata olives, olive oil, basil, vinegar, rosemary, capers, garlic, oregano, red pepper flakes, salt, and black pepper together in a large bowl.

Nutrition Facts

Per Serving: 258 calories; 18.5 g fat; 19 g carbohydrates; 5.6 g protein; 11 mg cholesterol; 540 mg sodium.

Tomato Cucumber Onion Salad

Ingredients

25 m 4 servings 266 cals

- 1 cup diced cucumber
- 1 cup diced fresh tomato
- 1/2 cup olive oil
- 1/2 cup red wine vinegar
- 1/4 cup diced red onion
- 1 teaspoon white pepper
- 1 teaspoon salt, or to taste

Directions

Prep 15 m Ready In 25 m

- Toss cucumber, tomato, olive oil, red wine vinegar, red onion, and white pepper together in a large bowl; season with salt. Refrigerate until slightly chilled, 10 to 15 minutes.

Nutrition Facts

Per Serving: 266 calories; 27.1 g fat; 6.5 g carbohydrates; 0.8 g protein; 0 mg cholesterol; 585 mg sodium.

Tomato Cucumber Salad with Mint

Ingredients

1 h 15 m 6 servings 88 cals

- 1/3 cup red wine vinegar
- 1 tablespoon white sugar
- 1 teaspoon salt
- 2 large cucumbers, peeled, seeded, and cut into 1/2-inch slices
- 3 large tomatoes, seeded and chopped
- 2/3 cup chopped red onion
- 1/2 cup chopped fresh mint
- 2 tablespoons olive oil
- salt and pepper to taste

Directions

Prep 15 m Cook 1 h Ready In 1 h 15 m

- In a large bowl, combine vinegar, sugar, and salt. Mix in cucumbers, and marinate 1 hour, stirring occasionally.
- Gently toss tomatoes, onion, mint, and olive oil with the marinated cucumbers. Season with salt and pepper.

Nutrition Facts

Per Serving: 88 calories; 4.8 g fat; 11.4 g carbohydrates; 1.6 g protein; 0 mg cholesterol; 395 mg sodium.

Carmel's Crunchy Pea Salad

Ingredients

30 m 6 servings 292 cals

- 8 slices bacon
- 1 (10 ounce) package frozen green peas, thawed and drained
- 1/2 cup chopped celery
- 1/2 cup chopped green onions
- 2/3 cup sour cream
- 1 cup chopped cashews
- salt and pepper to taste

Directions

Prep 15 m Cook 15 m Ready In 30 m

- Place bacon in a large, deep skillet. Cook over medium high heat until evenly brown. Drain, crumble and set aside.
- In a medium bowl, combine peas, celery, scallions and sour cream. Toss gently to mix.
- Just before serving, stir in cashews and bacon into salad. Season with salt and pepper.

Nutrition Facts

Per Serving: 292 calories; 21.2 g fat; 16.1 g carbohydrates; 11.5 g protein; 25 mg cholesterol; 503 mg sodium.

Apple and Zucchini Salad

Ingredients

20 m 8 servings 122 cals

- 1 pound zucchini, diced
- 3 apples, diced
- 1/2 green bell pepper, diced
- 1/2 red onion, chopped
- 1/3 cup vegetable oil
- 2 tablespoons red wine vinegar
- 1 teaspoon white sugar
- 1 teaspoon dried basil
- 3/4 teaspoon salt
- 1/4 teaspoon ground black pepper

Directions

Prep 20 m Ready In 20 m

- Combine zucchini, apples, green bell pepper, and onion in a bowl.
- Whisk vegetable oil, vinegar, sugar, basil, salt, and black pepper together in a separate bowl; drizzle over zucchini-apple mixture. Toss to coat.

Footnotes

- Partner Tip
- Reynolds Aluminum foil can be used to keep food moist, cook it evenly, and make clean-up easier.

Nutrition Facts

Per Serving: 122 calories; 9.3 g fat; 10.4 g carbohydrates; 1 g protein; 0 mg cholesterol; 225 mg sodium.

Sauerkraut Salad

Ingredients

6 servings 577 cals

- 1 quart sauerkraut, drained
- 1 onion, chopped
- 2 stalks celery, chopped
- 1 green bell pepper, chopped
- 1 large carrots, chopped
- 1 (4 ounce) jar diced pimento peppers, drained
- 1 teaspoon mustard seed
- 1 1/2 cups white sugar
- 1 cup vegetable oil
- 1/2 cup cider vinegar

Directions

- In a large bowl, mix together sauerkraut, onion, celery, green bell pepper, carrot, pimientos, and mustard seed. Set aside this mixture.
- In a small saucepan, mix together sugar, oil, and vinegar. Bring to a boil. Remove from heat.
- Pour sugar mixture over salad, cover, and leave it in the refregerator for 2 days before serving.

Footnotes

- Partner Tip
- Reynolds Aluminum foil can be used to keep food moist, cook it evenly, and make clean-up easier.

Nutrition Facts

Per Serving: 577 calories; 37.2 g fat; 62.2 g carbohydrates; 2.4 g protein; 0 mg cholesterol; 1057 mg sodium.

Crisp Marinated Cucumbers

Ingredients

8 h 10 m 4 servings 116 cals

- 1/2 cup white vinegar
- 1/2 cup white sugar
- 1/2 teaspoon salt
- 1/4 teaspoon celery seed
- 2 cucumbers, sliced
- 1/4 cup sliced sweet onion

Directions

Prep 10 m Ready In 8 h 10 m

- Whisk vinegar, sugar, salt, and celery seed together in a large bowl; stir in cucumbers and onion. Cover and refrigerate overnight. Serve cold.

Nutrition Facts

Per Serving: 116 calories; 0.2 g fat; 29.4 g carbohydrates; 0.8 g protein; 0 mg cholesterol; 293 mg sodium.

My Big Fat Greek Salad

Ingredients

1 h 10 m 4 servings 352 cals

- 2 large English cucumbers
- 1 pinch kosher salt
- 2 cups cherry tomatoes
- 1/4 red onion
- 1/2 red bell pepper
- 1/2 cup pitted Kalamata olives
- 1/2 cup pitted green olives
- 2 tablespoons minced fresh oregano
- salt and freshly ground black pepper to taste
- 1 pinch cayenne pepper, or to taste
- 1/4 cup red wine vinegar, or to taste
- 1/3 cup olive oil, or to taste
- 1 (4 ounce) package feta cheese, diced, divided
- 1 teaspoon minced fresh oregano, or to taste

Directions

Prep 20 m Ready In 1 h 10 m

- Peel off a few strips of cucumber skin using a channel knife, creating a striped pattern. Cut cucumbers in half crosswise. Cut each half into quarters before cutting into 1/4- to 1/2-inch slices. Place into a colander; toss with some kosher salt and let sit for 10 to 15 minutes.
- Meanwhile, cut cherry tomatoes in half. Rinse cucumbers; drain thoroughly for 10 to 15 minutes more.
- While cucumbers are draining, slice onion thinly. Cut bell pepper into strips. Turn knife diagonally and cut strips into diamond-shaped pieces. Slice Kalamata and green olives.
- Combine cucumbers, tomatoes, onion, bell pepper, olives, and 2 tablespoons oregano in a bowl. Season with salt, black pepper, and cayenne. Sprinkle in vinegar and toss thoroughly. Drizzle in olive oil. Add about 2/3 of the feta cheese and toss again. Cover with plastic wrap and refrigerate for 30 to 60 minutes.
- Give the salad another mix. Taste and season as desired. Scatter remaining feta cheese on top and garnish with remaining oregano.

Footnotes

- Chef's Notes:
- If you need to make this the day before, I suggest making the dressing separately, and then mixing everything before the event. I think this should only be dressed about 30 to 60 minutes before service for maximum enjoyment, but that's just my approach, and some folks prefer an overnight marination.
- Use 1/2 teaspoon dried oregano if you don't have the fresh kind.
- Between 4 and 6 ounces of feta cheese work well here.

Nutrition Facts

Per Serving: 352 calories; 31.8 g fat; 12.9 g carbohydrates; 6.3 g protein; 25 mg cholesterol; 1250 mg sodium.

A Different Carrot Raisin Salad

Ingredients

15 m 6 servings 385 cals

- 3 large carrots, shredded
- 1 cup raisins
- 1 cup walnuts
- 1/4 cup finely chopped celery
- 2 tablespoons shredded coconut
- 1/2 cup mayonnaise
- 2 tablespoons sour cream
- 1 tablespoon cider vinegar
- 1/2 teaspoon white sugar
- 1/4 teaspoon salt

Directions

Prep 15 m Ready In 15 m

- In a medium bowl, combine shredded carrots, raisins, walnuts, celery, and coconut. Whisk together mayonnaise, sour cream, vinegar, sugar, and salt. Stir dressing into carrot mixture. Chill a few hours before serving.

Nutrition Facts

Per Serving: 385 calories; 30.1 g fat; 29.7 g carbohydrates; 4.7 g protein; 9 mg cholesterol; 237 mg sodium.

Raw Beet Salad

Ingredients

20 m 4 servings 89 cals

- 1 pound beets, grated
- 2 tablespoons balsamic vinegar
- 1 tablespoon extra-virgin olive oil
- 1 tablespoon finely chopped fresh parsley
- 1 large clove garlic, minced
- 2 teaspoons Dijon mustard
- 1/4 teaspoon sea salt
- 1/8 teaspoon freshly ground black pepper

Directions

Prep 20 m Ready In 20 m

- Combine beets, balsamic vinegar, olive oil, parsley, garlic, mustard, sea salt, and black pepper in a bowl.

Nutrition Facts

Per Serving: 89 calories; 3.6 g fat; 13 g carbohydrates; 2 g protein; 0 mg cholesterol; 264 mg sodium.

Broccoli Salad with Red Grapes, Bacon, and Sunflower Seeds

Ingredients

2 h 30 m 8 servings 327 cals

- 8 slices bacon
- 1/3 cup sunflower seed kernels
- 1 large head broccoli, cut into bite-size pieces
- 1/3 cup diced red onion
- 1 cup seedless red grapes, halved
- 1 cup mayonnaise
- 3 tablespoons apple cider vinegar
- 2 tablespoons white sugar

- ground black pepper to taste

Directions

Prep 20 m Cook 10 m Ready In 2 h 30 m

- Place bacon in a large skillet and cook over medium-high heat, turning occasionally, until evenly browned, about 10 minutes. Drain bacon slices on paper towels. Crumble 7 slices of bacon; mix with sunflower seeds in a resealable bag.
- Combine broccoli, onion, and grapes in a bowl.
- Crumble the remaining bacon slice. Whisk mayonnaise, vinegar, sugar, and black pepper together in a bowl; fold in the 1 slice crumbled bacon. Pour dressing over broccoli mixture; toss to coat evenly. Cover bowl with plastic wrap and refrigerate for flavors to blend, about 2 hours.
- Sprinkle bacon-sunflower seed mixture over salad before serving; mix well.

Footnotes

- Cook's Notes:
- We never substitute the red grapes with raisins and we always use apple cider vinegar for this recipe. However, we sometimes substitute the sunflower seeds with chopped pecans or toasted sliced almonds.
- Add the crumbled bacon and sunflower seeds when it's time to serve. If you hold off and wait, the bacon and sunflower seeds stay nice and crunchy therefore enhancing the overall texture and flavor. Mix well once added.
- Partner Tip
- Reynolds Aluminum foil can be used to keep food moist, cook it evenly, and make clean-up easier.

Nutrition Facts

Per Serving: 327 calories; 29 g fat; 12.5 g carbohydrates; 6.3 g protein; 20 mg cholesterol; 382 mg sodium.

Lemony Cucumbers

Ingredients

4 h 10 m 7 servings 27 cals

- 2 cucumbers, sliced
- 1/4 cup white wine vinegar
- 2 tablespoons white sugar
- 2 teaspoons celery seed
- 1/8 teaspoon ground black pepper
- 3/4 teaspoon salt
- 2 tablespoons chopped onion
- 1 tablespoon lemon juice

Directions

Prep 10 m Ready In 4 h 10 m

- In a mixing bowl, combine the cucumbers, vinegar, sugar, celery seed, pepper, salt, chopped onion and lemon juice. Toss, cover and chill for 4 hours.

Asian Pasta Salad with Beef, Broccoli and Bean Sprouts

Ingredients

8 servings 468 cals

Soy-Ginger Dressing:

- 3 medium garlic cloves, minced
- 6 tablespoons soy sauce
- 1 tablespoon rice wine vinegar
- 1 tablespoon sugar
- 1 tablespoon sesame oil
- 1 teaspoon ground ginger
- 3/4 teaspoon hot red pepper flakes
- 2 tablespoons mayonnaise
- 1/4 cup vegetable oil

Pasta Salad:

- 2 tablespoons salt
- 1 pound penne pasta
- 8 ounces broccoli florets
- 1 pound rare deli roast beef, sliced 1/8 inch thick and cut into bite-size strips
- 3 medium carrots, peeled and coarsely grated
- 1 medium red bell pepper, cut into bite-size strips
- 2 cups bean sprouts
- 3 green onions, thinly sliced
- 1/2 cup chopped roasted (or honey-roasted) peanuts
- 1/4 cup chopped fresh cilantro

Directions

- Mix garlic, soy sauce, vinegar, sugar, sesame oil, ginger, and pepper flakes in a 2-cup Pyrex measuring cup. Whisk in mayonnaise until smooth, then in a slow steady stream, whisk in oil to make an emulsified dressing; keep chilled until ready to toss with salad. Store in a clean jar with lid.
- Bring 1 gallon of water and 2 tablespoons of salt to boil in a large soup kettle. Add pasta and, using package times as a guide, boil, stirring frequently and adding broccoli the last 1 minute, until just tender. Drain thoroughly (do not rinse) and dump onto a large, lipped cookie sheet. Set aside while preparing remaining salad ingredients.

- Place all salad ingredients (except soy-ginger dressing) in a large bowl or transfer to a gallon-size zipper bag. (Can be covered and refrigerated several hours at this point). When ready to serve, add dressing; toss to coat and serve.

Nutrition Facts

Per Serving: 468 calories; 19.2 g fat; 53.7 g carbohydrates; 23.9 g protein; 29 mg cholesterol; 3120 mg sodium.

Easy Broccoli Salad

Ingredients

50 m 4 servings 223 cals

- 1 1/2 pounds fresh broccoli
- 3 cloves garlic, mashed into a paste
- 2 tablespoons lemon juice
- 2 tablespoons rice vinegar
- 1/2 teaspoon Dijon mustard
- 1 pinch red pepper flakes, or to taste
- 1 pinch salt and ground black pepper, or to taste
- 1/3 cup olive oil

Directions

Prep 15 m Cook 5 m Ready In 50 m

- Trim bottoms of broccoli stems and cut off broccoli heads; cut the broccoli heads into quarters. Peel broccoli stems and cut into quarters crosswise.
- Bring a large pot of lightly salted water to a boil; reduce heat to medium and cook broccoli until tender when cut with a paring knife but still slightly firm, 5 to 6 minutes.
- Transfer broccoli to a large bowl filled with cold water and chill to stop the cooking process. Drain well. Arrange broccoli in a colander with the florets facing down towards the holes of the colander and allow broccoli to drip for at least 30 minutes.
- Whisk together garlic, lemon juice, rice vinegar, Dijon mustard, red pepper flakes, salt, and black pepper together in a large serving bowl. Slowly drizzle in olive oil while whisking rapidly until the dressing is thick and creamy. Adjust salt, black pepper, and crushed red pepper flakes to taste.
- Toss broccoli with the dressing; let stand 5 to 10 minutes to marinate, then toss again. Can be refrigerated up to an hour if you want to serve the salad cold.

Footnotes

- Partner Tip
- Reynolds Aluminum foil can be used to keep food moist, cook it evenly, and make clean-up easier.

Nutrition Facts

Per Serving: 223 calories; 18.6 g fat; 12.9 g carbohydrates; 5 g protein; 0 mg cholesterol; 73 mg sodium.

Grilled Asparagus Salad

Ingredients

13 m 6 servings 110 cals

- 1/4 cup olive oil
- 1/8 cup lemon juice
- 12 fresh asparagus spears
- 6 cups fresh spinach leaves
- 1/8 cup grated Parmesan cheese
- 1 tablespoon seasoned slivered almonds

Directions

Prep 10 m Cook 3 m Ready In 13 m

- Preheat a grill for low heat. Combine the lemon juice and olive oil on a plate. Place asparagus on the plate, and roll around to coat.
- Grill asparagus for about 5 minutes, turning at least once, and brushing with the olive oil mixture. Remove from the grill, and place back onto the plate with the oil.
- In a large bowl, combine the spinach, Parmesan cheese, and slivered almonds. Cut asparagus into bite-size pieces, and add to the salad along with the lemon juice and oil from the plate. Toss to blend, then serve.

Nutrition Facts

Per Serving: 110 calories; 10.2 g fat; 3.4 g carbohydrates; 2.6 g protein; 1 mg cholesterol; 50 mg sodium.

Mexican Street Vendor Style Corn Salad

Ingredients

20 m 8 servings 140 cals

- 2 (15.25 ounce) cans whole kernel corn, undrained
- 1 tablespoon butter
- 2 tablespoons mayonnaise
- 1/4 cup grated cotija cheese
- 1 pinch ground red pepper to taste
- 2 tablespoons lime juice, or to taste
- 1 sprig cilantro for garnish

Directions

Prep 10 m Cook 10 m Ready In 20 m

- Pour the corn into a saucepan, and boil over high heat until hot. Drain well, and return to the saucepan. Stir in the butter, mayonnaise, and cotija cheese. Season to taste with ground red pepper and lime juice. Spoon into a serving dish, and garnish with a sprig of cilantro to serve.

Footnotes

- Cook's Note

  You can grate Cotija or you can dice it. I prefer the grated because it doesn't overpower the corn.

- Partner Tip

  Reynolds Aluminum foil can be used to keep food moist, cook it evenly, and make clean-up easier.

Nutrition Facts

Per Serving: 140 calories; 6.4 g fat; 20.7 g carbohydrates; 3.8 g protein; 9 mg cholesterol; 395 mg sodium.

Raw Veggie Picnic Salad

Ingredients

30 m 12 servings 359 cals

- 6 slices bacon
- 4 cups broccoli florets
- 1 cup chopped celery
- 1 (10 ounce) package frozen green peas, thawed
- 1 cup sweetened dried cranberries
- 1/2 cup chopped green onions
- 1 cup seedless green grapes
- 1 cup seedless red grapes
- 1/2 cup slivered almonds
- 1/4 cup white sugar
- 1 teaspoon salt
- 1/4 cup white wine vinegar
- 2 tablespoons grated onion
- 1/4 cup grated Parmesan cheese
- 1 1/2 cups mayonnaise

Directions

Prep 20 m Cook 10 m Ready In 30 m

- Place bacon in a skillet over medium high-heat, and cook until evenly brown. Drain, crumble and set aside.
- In a large bowl, toss together the bacon, broccoli, celery, peas, cranberries, green onions, green grapes, red grapes, and almonds. In a separate bowl, whisk together the sugar, salt, vinegar, grated onion, Parmesan cheese, and mayonnaise. Pour dressing over the salad. Gently toss to coat.

Nutrition Facts

Per Serving: 359 calories; 27 g fat; 25.2 g carbohydrates; 6.1 g protein; 17 mg cholesterol; 536 mg sodium.

Greek Salad, The Best!

Ingredients

30 m 8 servings 385 cals

- 1 cup olive oil
- 3 tablespoons red wine vinegar
- 3 tablespoons grated Parmesan cheese
- 2 tablespoons lemon juice
- 2 tablespoons finely chopped garlic
- 2 tablespoons dried oregano, or to taste
- 1 1/2 teaspoons dried basil
- 1 teaspoon salt, or to taste
- freshly ground black pepper to taste
- 2 heads romaine lettuce, chopped
- 2 large tomatoes, cut into wedges
- 1 large cucumber, cut into matchsticks
- 1 red onion, sliced
- 1 cup black olives
- 1/2 pound feta cheese, crumbled

Directions

Prep 30 m Ready In 30 m

- Blend olive oil, vinegar, Parmesan cheese, lemon juice, garlic, oregano, basil, salt, and black pepper together in a food processor until smooth.
- Combine romaine lettuce, tomatoes, cucumber, red onion, black olives, and feta cheese together in large bowl. Drizzle dressing over vegetable mixture; toss to coat.

Nutrition Facts

Per Serving: 385 calories; 36 g fat; 11.8 g carbohydrates; 7 g protein; 27 mg cholesterol; 800 mg sodium.

Sliced Tomatoes with Fresh Herb Dressing

Ingredients

1 h 10 m 8 servings 95 cals

- 4 large ripe tomatoes, sliced
- 1/4 cup olive oil

- 2 tablespoons chopped fresh thyme leaves
- 2 tablespoons chopped fresh oregano
- 2 tablespoons chopped fresh parsley
- 2 tablespoons chopped fresh chives
- 2 tablespoons minced garlic
- 1/4 cup freshly grated Parmesan cheese
- salt and ground black pepper to taste

Directions

Prep 10 m Ready In 1 h 10 m

- Arrange the tomato slices in a shallow casserole dish. Whisk together the olive oil, thyme, oregano, parsley, chives, and garlic in a small bowl. Add salt and pepper to taste. Pour herb mixture over the tomatoes, covering evenly. Top with Parmesan cheese. Cover, and refrigerate at least 1 hour before serving.

Nutrition Facts

Per Serving: 95 calories; 7.9 g fat; 4.8 g carbohydrates; 2.3 g protein; 3 mg cholesterol; 53 mg sodium.

Broccoli Cranberry Salad

Ingredients

25 m 8 servings 314 cals

- 6 strips bacon
- 1 cup mayonnaise
- 1/4 cup white sugar
- 2 tablespoons red wine vinegar
- 3 heads broccoli, finely chopped
- 1/2 cup chopped red onion
- 1/3 cup salted sunflower kernels, toasted
- 1/4 cup dried cranberries

Directions

Prep 15 m Cook 10 m Ready In 25 m

- Place the bacon in a large skillet and cook over medium-high heat, turning occasionally, until evenly browned, about 10 minutes. Drain bacon slices on paper towels and crumble.
- Whisk mayonnaise, vinegar, and sugar in a bowl; refrigerate until ready to combine with salad.
- Combine broccoli, onion, bacon, sunflower seeds, and cranberries in a large bowl. Drizzle mayonnaise dressing over broccoli mixture; toss to coat.

Footnotes

- Partner Tip
- Reynolds Aluminum foil can be used to keep food moist, cook it evenly, and make clean-up easier.

Nutrition Facts

Per Serving: 314 calories; 25.2 g fat; 19 g carbohydrates; 6.1 g protein; 18 mg cholesterol; 355 mg sodium.

Cucumber and Dill Pasta Salad

Ingredients

30 m 6 servings 203 cals

- 2 cups macaroni
- 2 cups cucumber - peeled, seeded and chopped
- 1 cup chopped tomatoes
- 1 cup low-fat sour cream
- 1/2 cup skim milk
- 1 tablespoon chopped fresh dill weed
- 1/2 teaspoon coarse ground black pepper
- 1/2 teaspoon salt
- 1 tablespoon distilled white vinegar

Directions

Prep 10 m Cook 12 m Ready In 30 m

- Cook pasta in boiling salted water until al dente. Drain, and rinse in cold water. Transfer noodles to a large bowl.
- In a separate bowl, mix together sour cream, milk, dill, vinegar, and salt and pepper. Set dressing aside.
- Mix cucumbers and tomatoes into the pasta. Pour in dressing, and mix thoroughly. Cover, and refrigerate at least 1 hour and preferably overnight. Stir just before serving.

Nutrition Facts

Per Serving: 203 calories; 5.5 g fat; 31.3 g carbohydrates; 7 g protein; 16 mg cholesterol; 224 mg sodium.

www.ingramcontent.com/pod-product-compliance
Lightning Source LLC
Chambersburg PA
CBHW080907160726
48000CB00009B/2893